T0302212

CyRM^{SM}

Mastering the Management of Cybersecurity

CYRM^{SM}

Mastering the Management of Cybersecurity

David X Martin

CRC Press
Taylor & Francis Group
Boca Raton London New York

CRC Press is an imprint of the
Taylor & Francis Group, an **informa** business

First Edition published 2021
by CRC Press
6000 Broken Sound Parkway NW, Suite 300, Boca Raton, FL 33487-2742

and by CRC Press
2 Park Square, Milton Park, Abingdon, Oxon, OX14 4RN

© 2021 Taylor & Francis Group, LLC

CRC Press is an imprint of Taylor & Francis Group, LLC

ISBN: 978-0-367-56531-2 (hbk)
ISBN: 978-0-367-75785-4 (pbk)
ISBN: 978-1-003-09823-2 (ebk)

Typeset in Caslon
by SPi Global, India

For my family,
who gives life to the world around me.

Contents

INTRODUCTION   1

CHAPTER 1.   THE CURRENT LANDSCAPE   5
              Note   11

PRONG 1: CyRM℠: CYBER RISK MANAGEMENT

CHAPTER 2.   GATHER INTELLIGENCE, ANTICIPATE RISK   15

CHAPTER 3.   BUILDING A MORE EFFECTIVE CYBERSECURITY DEFENSE   21
              Sound the Alarm   22
              Solve the Problem   23
              Recover and Remember   23
              Consider Methods to Transfer Cyber Risks   24

CHAPTER 4.   ALIGN CRITICAL DECISION-MAKING FOR IT VS. BUSINESS 25
              Recognize the Problem and Address It   26
              Take Action   27
              Manage the Alignment   28

CHAPTER 5.   CYBERSECURITY FOR SENIOR EXECUTIVES AND BOARD
              MEMBERS   29

PRONG 2: CYBERWELLNESS^SM

CHAPTER 6. CYBERWELLNESS^SM: A COMPANYWIDE APPROACH 49
Incident Response Plans 51
Penetration Testing 52
Tabletop Exercises 53
Public Relations and Legal Counsel 54
Establish Effective Governance 54
Ongoing Workforce Training and Development 54
Implement Management Processes for All Third-Party
  Vendors and Suppliers 55
Take a Step Back 56

**CHAPTER 7. CULTIVATE A STRONG CULTURE TO ENHANCE
CYBERSECURITY** 59
Data-Centric Security 60
  Get the Users Involved 60
  Engage Employees in Training Applications 61
  Make Diversity Part of the Security Culture 61

PRONG 3: CYBERSECURITY AS A BUSINESS STRATEGY

CHAPTER 8. TRUST WILL BECOME A COMPETITIVE ADVANTAGE 65

CHAPTER 9. CYRM^SM AS A VITAL BUSINESS STRATEGY 69

CHAPTER 10. HOW TO THINK ABOUT THE FUTURE 75
Making Better Decisions Regarding Risk 77
Assessment 77
Rules of the Game 78
Making Your Decision 79
Reevaluate 80
Emerging Threats 81
Use of Scenarios Based on Emerging Threats 82
Applying CyRM^SM 83
Notes 84

CONCLUSION 85

APPENDIX A GUIDING PRINCIPLES FOR CYBER RISK GOVERNANCE 89

APPENDIX B PRIMER ON CYBERSECURITY FOR BOARDS OF DIRECTORS 111

INDEX 137

INTRODUCTION

Back in the 1990s—seems like eons ago, doesn't it?—General Electric CEO Jack Welch told business leaders, "If you're not confused, you don't know what's going on." I've always liked that admonition, because thinking you've got a handle on things can lead to arrogance and complacency; confusion keeps you humble. And if you're humble, you're teachable. And being teachable—being aware that there are many things you don't know (and even more things you don't *know* that you don't know)—keeps you seeking new information and remaining open to opportunities, all while staying alert to new threats.

At that time, I was the enterprise risk manager for Citicorp, the largest financial institution in the world, and I understood that financial institutions were mirrors of their environment. If the economy in which we're doing business is doing well, our customers do well, and we do well. The opposite is also true—even if you have the best risk professionals in the business. So back then, my approach was to thoroughly understand the environments we were operating in and to keep a keen eye on inflection points—leading indicators to know where those environments were going. For example, when our private clients in our emerging markets business started to move their private wealth offshore, I saw this as a leading indicator that their local economy was headed in the wrong direction.

Back then, the rate of technological innovation was a leading indicator, so I hired MIT professor Tsutomu Shimomura to "ethically hack" the bank. A few days later he came to me and said, "You guys are an easy target. All someone has to do is bombard your call center. No customer will be able to call in, and you'll be out of business in no time." I was startled. I quickly realized that cybersecurity—just like every other risk—needs to be managed.

Fast-forward to today: public scrutiny (and in some cases outrage) after cyberattacks, together with actions by regulatory authorities, have made cybersecurity a key leadership responsibility. When things go wrong, whether in a major or minor way, the ability to quickly identify and respond to a problem will determine the company's ultimate recovery. Another major breach of cybersecurity will soon be in the news. The only question is how dramatic and costly that breach will be, and whether the full extent of the damage will ever be made public. Worse still, should hackers gain access to the financial records of a major national bank or important defense contractor, we'll quickly forget about the relatively insignificant attacks at retailers like Target and Home Depot.

What accounts for the increase in cybercrime? Three broad new security challenges have emerged.

First, there has been a previously unimaginable explosion in the amount of data, connections, transactions, and communications that has overloaded traditional data systems.

Second, institutions have lost the ability to effectively identify problems. Faster innovation cycles and a dizzying array of new products mean that most businesses find themselves unable to quickly recognize security breaches. Social networking systems, big data, cloud computing, mobile internet, and Internet of Things technologies are generating personal data streams that have made authorization and message filtration extraordinarily difficult.

Third, there's a lack of formal control mechanisms. In an environment where cybersecurity disruptions are becoming more pervasive and sophisticated, there are still no recognized standards for detection, response, remediation, and enterprise-wide communication. The management of these critical functions is often left to the IT department, which is usually directed to pursue outdated, hardened-shell strategies designed only to discourage penetration.

Armed with decades of experience as a leader in risk management, I examined this landscape, and it became clear to me that we need an information security model that continually assesses the validity, reliability, and value of the information it gathers. I developed and honed that security model into a process that I know can help companies avoid the worst pitfalls of a cyberattack. It's called cyber risk management, or CyRMˢᴹ.

CyRMˢᴹ is a new paradigm that approaches security as a business problem and aligns it with business needs. So, instead of viewing security as a technical problem handled by technical people, it uses an outcome-driven approach that balances investment and risk. Even further, instead of throwing money at the problem at the expense of executive engagement, it connects cybersecurity with business decision-making to impact business outcomes.

To effectively impact business outcomes, CyRM℠ needs to consist of three prongs:

1. **Risk Management:** It needs to apply the tenets of risk management to cybersecurity in order to take a broad view of risks across an organization to inform resource allocation, better manage risks, and enable accountability.

2. **CyberWellness℠:** It needs to encompass not only the firm as a whole, but also every employee who needs to be responsible for the risks they undertake. This requires an active process with cybersecurity—just like physical wellness programs in which the company takes an active approach to promoting employees' good health.

3. **Cybersecurity as a Business Strategy:** Cybersecurity needs to be repositioned for what it really is—a growth enabler, and not just designed to reduce operational risks by eliminating the dangers posed by viruses and hackers. It also needs to enhance product integrity, customer experience, operations regulatory compliance, brand reputation, and investor confidence.

This book lays out my approach to CyRM℠ and shows you—business leaders and IT managers alike—how to work together and succeed. Each chapter of this book tells you what you need to know about managing the current cybersecurity landscape. And each chapter ends with CyRM℠ Action Points—proactive steps you can take to prepare yourself and your company to survive and succeed. I'm looking forward to being your educator and guide as we delve into CyRM℠.

1

THE CURRENT LANDSCAPE

On September 7, 2017, one of the nation's largest credit monitoring agencies, Equifax, announced that more than 143 million customer accounts had been breached in what may be the most significant cyberattack to impact US consumers to date. The number of affected individuals has since risen to an estimated 147 million people[1]—all of whom likely had their names, Social Security numbers, birth dates, addresses, and driver's license numbers compromised in the attack.

Amid the Equifax controversy, the US Securities and Exchange Commission (SEC) made some striking disclosures of its own. Newly arrived SEC Chair Jay Clayton announced on September 20, 2017, that the SEC's own EDGAR filing system had been penetrated by cybercriminals months previously. This led to questions about the safety of such systems, as well as the risk of insider trading by individuals with advance knowledge of sensitive and nonpublic company information.

Since then, other recent high-profile cyberattacks have abounded. Much to the chagrin of fans of the popular television show *Game of Thrones*, the HBO television network was breached by a group that pilfered more than 1.5 terabytes of information, including show scripts and full episodes of several prominent shows. The *Guardian* revealed that Deloitte LLP, one of the "Big Four" accounting firms—whose advisory clients include large companies and government departments—had been the victim of a breach and had its internal email system compromised. Deloitte has since notified six of its clients whose information may have been "impacted" by the breach, and it has completed an internal investigation into the incident. It took Uber more than a year to admit it had been hacked. The rideshare company purportedly paid a "ransom" in exchange for a promise by the hackers to delete purloined data and keep the cyber incident quiet.

Large-scale data breaches continue to happen every year. In 2019, a few of the notable larger ones included those that happened at Capital One, Facebook, Quest Diagnostics, and First American. At Capital One, a single hacker gained access to more than 100 million customer accounts and credit card applications. Quest Diagnostics revealed that a user gained access to medical information of more than twelve million patients through a third-party vendor.

Approximately one year after the Cambridge Analytica scandal, Facebook admitted to unintentionally making public more than one million user emails. In an even larger breach, First American, a US real-estate title company, revealed that nearly 900 million records were compromised! In terms of ransomware attacks, 2019 was also a banner year.

In 2020, the Citizen Lab (associated with the University of Toronto) exposed a group of mercenary hackers dubbed "Dark Basin," based in New Delhi. These for-hire hackers went after Exxon and a German company called Wirecard. Hackers for hire provide services to clients looking to cause trouble from a distance—in a different jurisdiction with minimal friction and not much chance of getting caught.

In 2020 hackers broke into Lockheed Martin, one of the largest US defense contractors, by targeting remote workers. All hackers need to gain access to a company is one vulnerable point; once they find that, they can seize control of a whole network. Once they're in, they can steal data and secrets and even lock authorized users out of the network.

One of the biggest exposures for any company lies in the cloud. As supply chains become ever more complex, financial institutions rely on third parties to provide scale and agility. Third-party provides are often the vector that cyber intruders exploit to reach their intended target. This dramatically increases the attack surface—the constellation of opportunities available to hackers—that companies have to worry about. Trusting that third parties will attend to your security needs in the same manner you would isn't a prudent strategy. If you rely on a weak set of interfaces to interact with cloud services, security issues can arise concerning confidentiality, integrity, availability, and accountability.

Here are a few examples of problems that may arise with cloud technology. Attackers now have the ability to use your (or your employees') login information to remotely access sensitive data stored on the cloud; falsify and manipulate data through hijacked credentials; or inject malware, which gets embedded in the cloud servers. And, if operating in tandem, attackers can eavesdrop, compromise the integrity of sensitive information, and even steal data.

What's more, the services provided by third-party companies are elastic—in other words, there are different degrees or levels of service and security available in them. This fosters an inconsistent security model. Maybe you've heard of application programming interfaces (APIs). APIs are programming filters that give users the opportunity to customize features of their cloud services to fit business needs. A bank and a bakery, for example, have very different needs, and it benefits them to have specific data filters on their sites. While these programs are incredibly useful in the way they allow users to authenticate, provide access, and affect encryption, they also can create vulnerabilities. The biggest vulnerability of an API lies in the communication that takes place between applications—creating exploitable security risks and new attack surfaces.

Case in point: in January 2019, researchers revealed a design feature common in most modern microprocessors that could allow content—including encrypted data—to be read from memory using malicious JavaScript code. Two variations of this problem, called Meltdown and Spectre, permit side-channel attacks because they break down the isolation between applications. That bit of technical jargon is another way of saying that a growing attack surface means there's heightened risk!

Ready for more potential problems that accompany cloud technology? In a recent breach of an online bank, the attacker was a former employee of the third-party company that hosted the bank's site. The perpetrator allegedly used web application firewall credentials to obtain "privilege escalation," a phrase we use to mean access to information most aren't supposed to see. Another potential problem with the cloud includes accidental data wipes by service providers. This recently happened at one large online retailer. Typically, businesses don't have recovery plans for data stored on the cloud. Once data is lost, it's gone forever (if it's not backed up).

Whether the attack comes via the cloud or some other way, the frequency and seriousness of cyberattacks on organizations holding sensitive personal and proprietary data have increased dramatically year after year—with dollar losses resulting from these attacks now in the *billions*. This is true of both public and private organizations. These attacks are certainly damaging and costly to everyone affected.

Banks, retailers, defense contractors, Fortune 500 companies, entertainment companies, and regional governments—all of these have lately been victims of cyberattacks. This is just a precursor of more attacks to come. Many employees in America are now working from home, using personal laptops on unsecured internet connections to access work files that contain confidential information and personal data. This provides ample opportunity for hackers—that "attack surface" mentioned earlier. Every company's attack surface has dramatically widened, making them easier targets. CYFIRMA, a cyber intelligence firm, reported that cyberthreats related to the COVID-19 pandemic increased 600 percent between February and March of 2020.

So, now that I've got your attention, what should we—what should YOU—do about cyberattacks? The answer is definitely not to stick your head in the sand. If you and your company want to survive and thrive in this cyber landscape, you've got to get smart and comprehensive. You need to invest in and enhance your cyber risk management (CyRMˢᵐ)

Some people may think the US government can protect them from attacks. After all, our Army protects us from invasion. Why not protect us from cyber invasion? But here's the cold, hard truth: although the United States government is excellent at good old-fashioned military defense, it's unfortunately not so great at cyber defense. In the two decades since September 11th, we have ample evidence that our government is going to great lengths to protect us from physical attacks by foreign terrorists. But we have no such evidence that the government has acted to protect us from calamitous cyberattacks. All you have to do is look at the record.

Consider that in November 2014, the director of the National Security Agency and USCYBERCOM testified before Congress that he believed two to three foreign countries had the ability to shut down the delivery of power, water, and fuel across the US via a cyberattack. Think about that. More than five years ago, our government was notified that two or three different countries could effectively shut down our national infrastructure. This obviously would have disastrous effects on the country, yet there followed no words of assurance from the government that steps were being taken to prevent this from happening. Perhaps the threat was too theoretical, too intangible, and too existential.

And yet, a mere *four days* after that testimony, North Korea cyberattacked Sony, destroying proprietary information, as well as computer hardware. A state actor proved it could access and embarrass a giant, multinational company. In 2015, we learned that the US Office of Personnel Management (OPM), despite earlier warnings, allowed the Chinese government to steal highly detailed security-clearance background data forms for twenty-one million Americans. More recently, the NSA failed to adequately safeguard highly advanced, weaponized "zero-day" exploits it had developed. (Zero-day exploits are advanced cyberattack tools that are so quick and devastating they leave the victim with no time to discover them.) The result of the NSA's failure is that those exploits are now in the hands of malicious actors who are wreaking havoc worldwide. In 2020, a major cyberattack by a group backed by a foreign government penetrated multiple parts of the United States federal government leading to a series of data breaches.

Despite these attacks and repeated warnings from experts, the United States government hasn't passed stand-alone cybersecurity-related legislation since 2002. In 2002, we were all using America Online, and Gmail didn't exist! The most significant proposed (but unpassed) cybersecurity bill of recent years asks the private sector to share more of its data with the government. Why should companies willingly hand over sensitive data to the entity that was grossly derelict in securing OPM and NSA data that's arguably some of the most sensitive in its treasury of state secrets?

To add insult to injury, this legislative inaction is accompanied by an unwillingness to hold foreign governments accountable for cyber assaults on our citizens and businesses. Things like geography or army size—factors that traditionally protected this country—don't exist in cyberspace. Suddenly, much lesser countries can intrude directly into our energy, communication, and financial industries. Bad actors are continually designing new and ever more powerful malware to remotely manipulate and disrupt these sectors.

There's growing concern within the US intelligence community that foreign governments will cyber-invade financial institutions—not to steal money, but to pollute, destroy, and manipulate data. Cyberattacks by foreign intelligence services designed to create chaos in record keeping, transaction precision, and currency valuations could disrupt and destroy the public trust to such a degree that the stability of the entire financial system may come into play.

The prospect of a toxic mix of continual and widespread financial data corruption—along with a government seemingly powerless to prevent it—is clearly a massive destabilization threat that, in turn, ought to trigger urgent strategic planning in both the public and private sectors. Don't wait for government to modernize its policies. Don't blindly trust third-party companies. Cyber bad actors have incredible reach to massive numbers of potential victims. They change tactics rapidly and remain largely anonymous as they traverse a boundary-less digital realm, wreaking havoc from the comfort of their native lands.

The bad guys are met—when they can be met—by a US government lugging around its analog-era legal construct that divides by mission (law enforcement, intelligence, military) and geography (domestic, foreign, judicial districts, US Person, non-US Person), wielding policies and procedures largely constructed during the Cold War (security classification levels).

The government is clearly not adequate, strategic, or nimble in the face of new cyberthreat realities. It's high time to reexamine the sufficiency of current criminal law, international treaties and agreements, and governance protocols within the context of our now virtually interconnected planet. However, given the pathetic track record of government thus far, don't hold your breath waiting for it to get its act together. Act now.

Some people change when they see the light; others change only when they feel the heat. In other words: you can be proactive or you can be reactive. When it comes to cybersecurity, the United States government has proven to be reactive. It's incumbent upon smart business leaders—those who see the light—to take steps NOW to protect their companies. As attack surfaces multiply and government slowly responds, it's time for you to invest in CyRM^{SM} and take the lead in keeping the bad guys at bay.

CyRM^SM ACTION POINTS: UNDERSTANDING THE LANDSCAPE

- Develop an understanding of the recent cyberattacks on your industry and key competitors.
- Get familiar with the systems and software your company uses.
- Pay attention to routine alerts warning of cyber vulnerabilities in the company's systems and software.

Note

1 "Equifax Data Breach Settlement," Federal Trade Commission, https://www.ftc.gov/enforcement/cases-proceedings/refunds/ equifax-data-breach-settlement.

PRONG 1
CyRM℠:
Cyber Risk
Management

2

GATHER INTELLIGENCE, ANTICIPATE RISK

As we saw in Chapter 1, it's no longer a question of whether a company will be attacked, but more a question of *when* this will happen—and how the organization is going to prevent it. When things go wrong, whether in a major or minor way, the ability to quickly identify and respond to a problem will determine your company's ultimate recovery. My approach, CyRM℠, applies the tenets of risk management to cybersecurity. I believe it's essential to take a broad view of risks across an organization to inform resource allocation, better manage risks, and enable accountability. As with traditional risk management, the goal of CyRM℠ is to identify risks early and implement appropriate mitigations to prevent incidents or attenuate their impact. To foster an excellent cyber risk management program, you first need to understand the principles and practices of enterprise risk management.

Risk managers survey the landscape of risk a company faces in a variety of ways and then create appropriate responses based on those risks. A helpful analogy in considering risk management is the human body: your five senses receive stimuli and convey data to your brain in order to spot potential dangers and anticipate problems. Historical memory helps you predict potential outcomes based on past experiences and helps you plan potential responses. Your five forward-looking senses, coupled with your historical memory, are continuously monitoring your immediate environment to alert you to potential danger. For example, the smell of smoke and/or the heat of an approaching fire tells you how imminent and how severe your risk is of being harmed by the fire. The sharper your senses, the more quickly your body can react to protect itself. Your organization's risk management system should be continuously sensing any potential risks ahead, determining how serious they are to your business, and providing effective mechanisms to respond quickly.

For the more technically minded reader, another apt metaphor is radar. What's unique about radar is that while it uses historical performance—not unlike your body's historical memory—it also looks forward to predict a future outcome.

Here's how it works: the radar antenna transmits radio waves that bounce off any object in their path. The bounced-back energy returns to a dish that determines the object's range, altitude, direction, and/ or speed. Tracking algorithms predict future positions of the moving object. These algorithms are, for the most part, based on historical performance, with frequent forward-facing updates. In other words, radar is very good at both gathering intelligence *and* anticipating risk.

Risk management—like radar—relies on quantifiable data. There's an inverse correlation between risk and information. The less information you have, the higher the risk you run. Consider a simple everyday example: if you don't know the weather forecast, you increase the risk of dressing inappropriately and getting caught unprepared in a downpour.

From a risk management perspective, risk and uncertainty are quantifiable based on whether the probabilities of occurrence and possible outcomes are known. The resulting potential loss amount can be easily calculated. For example, if the weather forecast says there's 100 percent probability of rain, but you don't carry an umbrella and your new shoes get ruined, the potential loss amount is the cost of buying a new pair of shoes. If there were several possible outcomes/costs resulting from ruining your shoes in the rain—the cost of replacing them, or taking them to a shoemaker to try to restore them—you could compute a potential loss amount based on all possible outcomes/costs.

Taking this simple example one step further, suppose you decide to take your shoes off in the rain to keep from ruining them; you have no idea what might happen to your feet. One approach would be to develop scenarios to determine what possibly could happen to your feet, the probabilities of each type of damage, and computing the potential loss amount. The problem becomes even more difficult to solve when you don't know what could possibly happen to your feet from walking barefoot in the rain.

The problem takes on a totally different dimension if you're walking without shoes in the rain across the deck of a ship at sea—because no rational individual wants to leave survival to probabilities. In other words, it's no longer a question of managing *uncertainty*—it becomes a question of *survival*. Your thought process switches from "Are the costs reasonable for the risks I'm assuming?" to "This is a risk I'm just not willing to assume. Are the protections I have in place adequate for me to not get seriously hurt?" In other words: *At what point does the line that you're not willing to cross become about survival—about your very existence—and no longer about simply quantifying the cost?*

Many risk managers work with scenarios on issues related to survivability to try to bind the realm of possibilities. Scenarios have limitations: they only address *known unknown* risks (things that you can imagine), but consequently don't address what you do *not* know (the *unknown unknown* risks). A good risk manager asks, "How do I turn as many unknown risks into known risks, which can then be quantified?"

For example, consider again the scenario of a person walking without shoes across a slippery, rain-drenched deck of a ship at sea. What if the rain was from a hurricane, where in many cases the strength of the winds or height of the incoming water (all velocity-related) are underestimated and cause knock-on effects? Not only can you slip and fall overboard—what about the scenario of the boat capsizing and the rescue party ashore not being able to mobilize to save you?

As with radar, there are sophisticated formulas that help risk officers quantify all these scenarios. Intelligence is gathered (with the help of these formulas) and risk is anticipated.

The evolution of cyber risk management into an effective oversight role has been hampered by most organizations' inability to organize, classify, and *measure* cyber risks the way they would handle other kinds of risk. *The quantification of cybersecurity risk should be at the heart of cyber risk management.* Quantifying cyber risk leads to better decisions, because it describes risk in the same common language or context of other risks in the company. The reporting of cyber risk to senior executives, the board of directors, and other stakeholders facilitates a better understanding of the level of cyber risk over time for the company, specific businesses, products, and activities.

Sounder decisions can also be made regarding the overall cybersecurity budget and the allocation of the cybersecurity spend, as well as on insurance coverage. It also helps to create a culture in which vulnerabilities are taken seriously. It provides an objective assessment of third-party vendors. It helps facilitate the integration of cyber risk with other enterprise and operational risks.

So, how does a cyber risk manager gather intelligence and anticipate risk? There are seemingly infinite unknowns in the cyber landscape. I would suggest that an innovative approach based on the manufacturing industry can be used to address cybersecurity operational disruptions for organizations of all types.

For example, in manufacturing, consider the assembly line at an auto manufacturing plant. If a disgruntled employee fires a bazooka at the middle of an assembly line, the plant management team can determine how long it will take to repair the line, how much it will cost to repair, and the cost of lost production. In other words, by focusing on *what* happened, irrespective of *how* it happened, the auto manufacturer can determine the potential disruption loss from the bazooka. (Of course, this scenario should also lead to an additional analysis of the risks generated by poor plant morale and disgruntled employees. But you get the point.)

Let's extend this example to an online banking application that's supposed to be operational 24/7. Suddenly, in the middle of the night on a three-day holiday weekend, the banking app is rendered useless by a cyberattack. Irrespective of *how* the attack happened, and by focusing solely on *what* happened, the bank can determine the critical nodes that need to be repaired, how much it will cost, how long it will take, and the cost of the downtime—all of which can be *quantified*, just like in the manufacturing example.

This approach, which focuses on the impact of a service disruption regardless of what caused it, allows you to effectively create a disruption model that you can use to quantify cybersecurity risk related to operational disruptions. Bottom line: cyber risk managers should focus on critical disruption nodes to improve resiliency—long before an attack ever happens.

As with the classic risk example of walking in the rain, cyber risk managers often overlook the knock-on effects in these scenarios. As an example, let's say a cyberattack on the financial system in New York includes an attack on the Manhattan power grid over a weekend. The financial exchanges all have emergency power systems, but their responses could be hampered because subways would also be out of commission. The knock-on effect is that the technical people who are supposed to respond to the attack would have great difficulty making it into the city—a fact that could easily be overlooked.

A good cyber risk management officer focuses on *what* disruptions could happen, not on *how* they could happen. It's also important to consider the knock-on effects of risk. And, ultimately, a good cyber risk manager must ask: "Are the protections I have in place adequate for my survivability?"

Take, for example, a truly unknowable risk, such as the total amount of reputational loss created by a cyber incident. The operative question is: "What are the best practices—a response plan and policies—that should be developed so that the impact can be absorbed and the organization can continue to function?"

In these cases, it's important to know what the "crown jewels" of the company are, then to put down bright lines and strong mitigating controls to protect them. For example, in an asset management company, personal client data is extremely sensitive and may require extra layers of controls, including different security protocols. A second-line cyber risk management perspective should be primarily: "is the company doing everything it needs to do to properly mitigate the impact of these risks to ensure sustainability?"

A strong CyRM℠ approach does the following:

- Focuses on the *impact* of the cybersecurity events—not *how* they happen.
- Uses disruption models to quantify operational disruptions.
- Converts as many unknown risks into known risks, so they can be quantified.
- And, for those truly unknowable risks, focuses on what needs to be done to ensure survivability.

CyRM℠ ACTION POINTS: GATHER INTELLIGENCE

- Engage key cybersecurity personnel.
- Evaluate the existing cybersecurity risks, and prioritize.
- Ensure they have appropriate systems in place to escalate information about potential cyber incidents.
- Develop systems to monitor cybersecurity efforts.

3

BUILDING A MORE EFFECTIVE CYBERSECURITY DEFENSE

Think of the cyber risk management prong of CyRM℠ like the human immune system. When a germ breaches the body's natural barriers, the immune system mounts a three-step defense: sound the alarm, solve the problem, and recover and remember. The first defenders on the scene are the white blood cells, which constantly circulate throughout the body, much like police on patrol. Next, specialized white blood cells called lymphocytes engage in a two-pronged attack—one directed at infected cells and the other at hostile microbes roaming through the blood. Finally, once the invaders and the compromised cells have been destroyed, the immune system's soldiers return to their bases, leaving a smaller number of seasoned veterans to attack should the invader return.

The effectiveness of cybersecurity defense, like that of the immune system, depends largely on each component efficiently fulfilling its role. Corporations clearly need to manage cybersecurity at the enterprise level and must improve the ability of each element—line management, operations, internal audit, risk, and compliance—to satisfy its individual and organizational functions. Managing cybersecurity risks requires three lines of defense. The first is to prevent cyber incidents from occurring and to protect the organization. This is the responsibility of everyone in the entire organization, and especially the technology and information security departments. Senior management should designate a senior partner who's the responsible officer for firmwide cybersecurity. In the day-to-day management of technology or in a crisis, it's far better to have a skillful leader rather than a subject matter expert. In choosing the right person, his or her leadership skills—communication and crisis management—are equally important. CyRM℠ isn't managed in a silo. Discussions should be part and parcel of all management processes, such as new product approvals, merger due diligence, and third-party outsourcing arrangements.

The second line of defense is providing independent oversight to ensure that risks are actively and appropriately managed. Those who are most intimately involved in cybersecurity may occasionally miss things because they're in the trenches every day. The risk management department should provide this independent, objective perspective—a fresh pair of eyes or a constructive challenge, if you will. The risk management staff should be playing the same role and performing the same functions as they do for all other risks within the company. For example, they should play a key role in determining what the "crown jewels" are of the company that need to be protected, then evaluating whether the controls in place are appropriate.

The third line of cybersecurity defense is the audit function, which periodically tests the policies and controls that are in place to ensure they're in position and effective. Internal audit should play a critical role in helping the company manage cyberthreats by providing an independent assessment of existing and needed controls, as well as helping senior management understand and address the many diverse risks in today's digital world. Internal audit should also evaluate the full cybersecurity framework rather than cherry-picking items. This evaluation involves understanding the current state against framework characteristics, where the organization is going, and the minimum expected cybersecurity practices across the industry or business sector. The initial assessment should inform further, more in-depth reviews. It isn't intended to be an exhaustive analysis requiring extensive testing. Rather, the initial assessment should drive additional risk-based cybersecurity deep-dive reviews.

The following is a summary of the key components of building a CyRMˢᴹ immune system, which are discussed in greater detail in subsequent chapters.

Sound the Alarm

Smart network surveillance, early warning indicators, multiple layers of defense, and lessons from past events are all critical components of true cyber resilience. Cybersecurity cannot be guaranteed, but a timely and appropriate reaction can.

Be aware of the risks posed when third parties handle sensitive company data, as third parties can be impactful to an operating environment. Companies aren't usually as attuned to cybersecurity risks from third parties as they are for their own businesses, even though third parties can create the same adverse, long-term effects.

For example, the sharing of data and communication between the company and its vendors is no longer fully in control of the internal operations of the company, as these external parties create new entry points into a company's technology environment, adding complexity and potential volatility to the operating environment. Basics for a third-party program should include third-party exposures prioritized based on risk (including cyber) to the organization; clear assessment tools in place for the onboarding of any new relationships; and ongoing, risk-adjusted monitoring processes in place to assess adherence to contract terms and joint disaster recovery testing with primary service providers.

Solve the Problem

Develop the organizational understanding to manage cybersecurity risk to systems, assets, data, and capabilities. When things do go wrong—because sooner or later, they will—the ability to quickly identify the problem will lead to a more effective recovery.

Develop and implement appropriate safeguards to ensure delivery of critical infrastructure services. It's also important to leverage emerging open-source intelligence services and to use the data gathered to guide ongoing cybersecurity investment. Over time, that data will be pooled, allowing new tools to be developed to analyze, prevent, and mitigate the cyberthreat of the day. This new intelligence will be particularly valuable when proactively quantifying risks and evaluating the investment levels required to protect specific assets.

Recover and Remember

Develop and implement the appropriate activities to maintain plans for resilience and to restore any capabilities or services that were impaired due to a cybersecurity event. Just like subjecting oneself to an annual medical examination, so, too, senior management must institute independent cybersecurity review processes. Threats should be viewed in the context of tolerance levels—high and low—and treated accordingly. A comprehensive management framework for cybersecurity should encompass governance, the setting of objectives, prompt identification of rapid events, risk assessment, and response and control activities.

Consider Methods to Transfer Cyber Risks

Legal and other practical considerations can (and should) be employed to partition and mitigate the risk. However, the risk—no matter where it originates—will rebound to your company in times of crisis or stress. Feeling reasonably secure about your company's CyRM℠ program isn't just a matter of being able to answer questions like, "Does our company have the right governance structure?" Rather, it's also being able to answer bigger questions, such as, "Are we thinking about security the right way, and where is all this going?"

CyRM℠ ACTION POINTS: BUILDING A SOLID DEFENSE

- Determine the most valuable assets and seek effective strategies to protect them.
- Develop the organizational understanding to manage cybersecurity risk to systems, assets, data, and capabilities.
- Develop and implement appropriate safeguards to ensure delivery of critical infrastructure services.
- Be aware of the risks posed when third parties handle sensitive company data.
- Develop and implement appropriate activities to maintain plans for resilience and to restore any capabilities or services that were impaired due to a cybersecurity event.
- Evaluate risk management strategies.
- Consider methods to transfer cyber risks.

4

ALIGN CRITICAL
DECISION-MAKING FOR
IT vs. BUSINESS

Today's board directors face an important question in reviewing technology decisions: Is the company's IT decision-making aligned with its strategic business decision-making? Unfortunately, this key alignment is absent in most companies today. A company that wants to implement a robust CyRM℠ policy must ask itself the following three questions to evaluate the alignment between IT and business strategy:

- Is technology leveraged to produce demonstrable value to the business in terms of productivity, business and revenue goals, business agility, improvement of the client experience, speed to market, and co-adopting with customers?
- Is generating business value from IT a shared responsibility demonstrated by IT being frequent partners in setting the strategic direction; being thought of as innovators instead of simply service providers; and working closely with the business units to leverage emerging technologies?
- Is there a continual process of adjusting IT capabilities across multiple dimensions and critical time frames that includes the effective exchange of ideas, knowledge, and information between IT and business, leveraging the IT infrastructure to support new applications, a shift in emphasis to data and security, and the mutual rating of projects against a finite set of value criteria?

Board members need to consider the following steps in evaluating the misalignment between strategic and operational decision-making and IT decision-making in their organizations. The problem is misalignment; the goal is alignment. It's senior management's job to manage this alignment on an ongoing basis:

1. Recognize the problem—or opportunity—and address it.
2. Gather information and develop alternative approaches.
3. Choose the alternative you think will be most successful.
4. Act based on your decision.

Recognize the Problem and Address It

In far too many organizations today, IT strategy is an afterthought—bolted on to the business strategy rather than becoming an integral part of it. This is what leads to misalignments between a company's strategic and operational business decisions and their IT decisions. Despite the important role IT strategy should be playing in product and business strategy today, too often it isn't. So, the first step is to identify this misalignment as the problem—then determine that it's being addressed as such. Senior management should keep their eye on the goal. That goal is alignment.

If the business makes technology decisions without the IT department's input, or IT makes business decisions without including senior management's business goals, alignment is impossible. As business needs and organizational priorities change, the senior management team will react by developing strategies that work for them, but they'll give little thought to including IT in supporting these changes.

Each department and senior executive sees business problems—and opportunities—through their own functional perspective. Alignment is no exception. Unfortunately, functional silos often fail to communicate and share their perspectives with one another. Board members should be in the unique position to see the big picture—and to evaluate whether everyone's role, including IT's, is clear to all.

In making good decisions, one needs to gather information that's pertinent to the problem. It's important to cast a wide net in order to fully comprehend both the importance and the urgency of the problem. Gathering plenty of information from a variety of sources will also help generate ideas for potential solutions.

It's important not to evaluate potential solutions too soon in the process. Sometimes ideas that seem off the wall or crazy at first turn out to be great possibilities upon further consideration. Management guru Peter Drucker used to say, "Organizations need two kinds of people: bureaucrats and lunatics. Innovation always comes from the lunatics—never the bureaucrats." So be sure to determine that senior management is consulting with the company's "wild and crazy guys" as they solicit ideas for possible solutions.

In evaluating senior management's options for action, you need to determine how a potential decision will effect everyone else involved. Ask yourself: "What are the likely results of this decision? How will it affect the business now? And how will it affect it in the future?"

Caution: an IT department's answers to these questions can sometimes be confusing. There are words and terms that are part of the information security culture that don't easily translate to people without a deep industry background. Further, IT staff have a predisposition toward focusing on technology versus nontechnology factors when there's a problem to address. When issues come up— as they do at an incredible rate in IT—they assume they're either technology-related or can be solved with technology or sequentially, which is how most IT issues are resolved.

Take Action

Once you've evaluated options and are comfortable with senior management's decision, it's important to evaluate whether everyone required takes action. It's critical for senior management to continually evaluate the decision and the actions that have been taken to ensure that everything is working as planned. This step is also fundamental because it may require senior management to seek out new information and make adjustments and further changes along the way.

IT risks are measured and evaluated differently from business risks, which impacts the decision-making process. IT risk is measured in terms of performance, cost, or time to implement. When decisions concerning the appropriate level of service are made by IT, they're likely to opt for the highest levels of service—because IT is usually judged on performance reliability.

Whereas generating real business value requires different metrics to determine success—and the highest level of service may not be required. Since IT allocates its costs, it often needs to track and manage costs differently, which can cause profound disconnects.

Manage the Alignment

It's important for board members to assess whether:

- IT leaders are given the opportunity to change their department's role from "service provider" to one of a "trusted partner"—becoming stakeholders making the business successful.
- IT strategy is developed in a broader business context that understands and keep track of how IT services are supporting business objectives.
- The company's leadership team reviews IT strategy alongside business strategy to determine how technology is helping or hindering growth. Key things to keep in mind:

  - IT-related decisions shouldn't be made in isolation by technologists, nor without knowing the business alternatives and trade-offs.
  - IT strategy should be a continuation of the business strategy, which requires an ongoing dialogue to clarify business needs in business terms.
  - The impact of IT on a company's business strategy requires knowledge of the business to properly weigh critical business trade-offs.

In short, to compete effectively in today's technology-driven world, companies need to get the alignment right.

CyRMˢᴹ ACTION POINTS: ALIGN CRITICAL DECISION MAKING FOR IT VS. BUSINESS

- Review cybersecurity budget for appropriateness.
- Assess whether the IT vs. business alignment is right in terms of roles, business strategy, interactions, and trade-offs.

5

CYBERSECURITY FOR SENIOR EXECUTIVES AND BOARD MEMBERS

Although cybersecurity isn't a new challenge for boards of directors, the sheer scope and volume of recent events suggest that we may be experiencing a watershed moment when it comes to directors' responsibility to oversee—and managers' duty to implement—adequate cybersecurity systems at companies. Following Equifax's public disclosure of the cyberattack affecting its systems in 2017, observers learned a good deal about what potentially went wrong at the company—including a series of red flags that senior managers and boards of directors at other companies may learn from. Indeed, the recent breaches at many companies reveal a series of lessons and warnings that boards of directors simply cannot afford to overlook anymore.

The first lesson is that companies must pay attention to routine alerts warning of cyber vulnerabilities in the company's systems and in software the company uses. Think back to the examples of high-profile cyberattacks I referenced in Chapter 1: Equifax, Uber, HBO, and Deloitte. In Equifax's case, hackers apparently exploited a known network vulnerability in the Apache Struts web-application software, which Equifax used to build its web applications. The US Department of Homeland Security's United States Computer Emergency Readiness Team ("US-CERT") notified Equifax and many others of this vulnerability and the need to patch the software on March 8, 2017. Although the company disseminated the US-CERT notification internally by email and requested that appropriate personnel apply the patch, the patch was apparently not installed, or not installed correctly, and follow-on scans of the system one week later failed to reveal the error. A good CyRM℠ protocol regularly checks those alerts.

The second lesson for board members is that companies must ensure they have appropriate systems in place to escalate information about potential cyber incidents. For example, does the general counsel have a process for imposing a freeze on trading in the company's securities by individuals with insider knowledge of material breaches during key windows of time? In Equifax's case, it was revealed that several executives had traded in the company's stock after the breach had been reported internally, but before the public had knowledge of the breach. This raised questions about possible insider trading and a lack of internal controls at a time when Equifax was already subject to intense public scrutiny over the breach itself. (The executives have since been cleared of wrongdoing by a special committee at Equifax tasked with analyzing the breach.)

The third lesson is that boards of directors must have a public response plan in place should a catastrophic cyberattack occur on their watch. Equifax's public handling of the incident has been widely criticized from virtually all angles. Many, for example, have complained that it took the company a full month to disclose the incident publicly after the company first learned of the breach in late July 2017. Others have ridiculed Equifax for directing consumers in the immediate aftermath of the breach to an insecure "spoofed" website mimicking the one Equifax had set up to engage with customers anxious to learn if their personal information had been compromised. Still others lamented that the company appeared to be in "PR mode" following the breach, making missteps such as offering credit monitoring services to affected individuals for a fee, rather than free of charge. Later, Equifax moved to offer victims free access to credit monitoring services, but it forced those customers to agree to lengthy arbitration provisions that would limit the customers' ability to sue the company in connection with the services. Equifax later abandoned the arbitration clause after a public outcry.

All of these events suggest that Equifax was ill-prepared to deal with the public fallout that would predictably ensue following a disclosure of this magnitude. A good CyRM℠ plan is prepared for any eventuality.

The fourth lesson for board members is that companies should carefully consider when and how they'll disclose a breach. The disclosures of cyber incidents at Equifax and Uber provide valuable guidance to boards of directors in this regard. A company must consider not only its legal disclosure obligations, but also the court of public opinion when assessing when, and what, to disclose. In a similar vein, some have pointed out that the SEC's public disclosure of a cyber incident involving its EDGAR database came months after internal reports of the event were raised, illuminating just how difficult it is for any actor—including those charged with overseeing disclosure-based conduct—to balance the competing needs for a speedy public disclosure and a thorough internal review. The SEC's own less-than-ideal response to a cyber breach (and a resulting delayed cyber disclosure) raises questions about how the agency will pursue companies for cyber-related disclosures in the future and balance the competing needs for prompt disclosures on one hand, and rigorous internal reviews on the other.

A final lesson is that companies should be aware of the risks posed when third parties handle sensitive company data. The events at Deloitte provide yet another data point and reinforce the notion that companies must be concerned not only with their own cybersecurity systems, but also those of third-party vendors and consultants (and even, perhaps, the government) when those entities handle sensitive company data.

Learning the lessons I list above is only half the battle. Once senior executives and board members understand these lessons, it's essential to implement an effective and dynamic cybersecurity program at their company. The following considerations will also help a director test the current status and effectiveness of the cybersecurity program.

As a first principle, directors should understand their fiduciary duties when it comes to cybersecurity and the overarching legal terrain guiding their companies. In addition to business and reputational risks, a lapse in cybersecurity can result in significant legal consequences for a company, its management, and, in certain cases, its board of directors. Companies must be aware of and understand various federal and state statutes, some of which regulate specific industries or types of sensitive information. Companies must also be aware that federal and state regulators, such as the SEC, DOJ, and FTC, may increasingly focus on cybersecurity when enforcing otherwise non-cyber-specific laws, such as federal consumer protection and securities laws. In addition, directors must also heed the risk of shareholder and consumer lawsuits, which are commonly initiated in the wake of the disclosure of cybersecurity incidents. As discussed below, the company's general counsel and internal cyber personnel should schedule regular briefings for the board to assess these developments.

Cybersecurity is a "first order" risk in many industries. If they haven't already done so, boards of directors should invest in a formal briefing to discuss the range of existing cybersecurity risks facing their companies and weigh the pros and cons of various mechanisms that may help protect the company's most valuable assets in light of those risks.

The board should first identify the company's most valuable assets and evaluate how those assets might be compromised by a cyber incident. For some companies, their most valuable asset is customers' private financial information, personally identifiable information, or possibly health records. For others, it might be intellectual property, or perhaps a proprietary database, or even a cache of sensitive emails. Any cybersecurity program must be geared toward protecting these most important corporate assets.

Directors should have a baseline understanding of the various types of cyber breaches that may occur on company systems and be familiar with the technical terms frequently used in the industry. Common cyber incidents at companies may range from malware to phishing attacks, and from unpatched software vulnerabilities to advanced persistent threats ("APTs"). Additionally, vulnerabilities in a company's physical security may allow actors to penetrate the company's cyber defenses.

While it isn't necessarily incumbent on the board to study the technical mechanisms of a cyberattack or response thereto, the board should have enough familiarity with these concepts to enable productive discussions with management and effective oversight of the company's cybersecurity program. In taking stock of existing cybersecurity risks, boards should pay close attention to trends and recent events in their particular industry and those impacting companies of a similar size. Particular types of cyberattacks appear more frequently in some industries and less in others. If you're a small retailer, for example, your most pressing cybersecurity concern may be point-of-sale intrusions, where attackers exploit weaknesses in remote-access applications (often provided by third-party vendors) in order to siphon your customers' credit card payment information. On the other hand, if you're a large financial institution with sprawling and accessible physical infrastructure (e.g., ATM machines), then you may face a broader range of cyber vulnerabilities, including the risk of "skimming" attacks on individual nodes in the network.

Directors should also have a broad understanding of who or which groups are most likely to target their companies, and for what purpose. As a starting point, the "2017 Data Breach Investigations Report" by Verizon suggests that the majority of cyber breaches are perpetrated by external threat actors (75 percent), while a smaller percentage are perpetrated by insiders, such as employees or former employees (25 percent). A growing number of breaches can be traced to state-affiliated actors (18 percent), while a smaller percentage involves business partners (2 percent).

Once the board has a good handle on the company's existing cyberthreat profile, it should prioritize strategies to mitigate the risk of an actual cyber breach. An effective director will help the company determine which assets are most valuable and evaluate the key controls in place to protect them.

He or she will also plan for contingencies and ensure there's an appropriate response framework in place to deal with potential cyber incidents. Part of this exercise will inevitably entail reviewing the company's budget related to cybersecurity to determine whether it's appropriate in light of existing threats and the robustness of existing company systems. (Keep in mind that it's less expensive to prevent a problem than it is to fix it.)

One key takeaway is that there are no offensive strategies in cybersecurity—only defensive strategies. In addition, you can't protect everything. Even the most technologically advanced organization in cyber—the National Security Agency (NSA)—couldn't protect its deepest secrets. It's therefore critical for the company to (1) reflect on which company assets are most valuable; (2) determine which systems are most vulnerable; and (3) consider what available mechanisms and strategies are both business-critical and cost-effective in view of this calculus.

Firms that really "get it" when it comes to great CyRM℠ plans have adaptive cultures. However, most corporate cultures don't change quickly—they evolve at a slow pace. As a result, the security culture in many organizations hasn't kept pace with the threat landscape in which they operate.

Security needs to be framed as a critical enabler that helps the company deliver its promise to customers. It also needs to be viewed by all levels of the company's workforce as a shared endeavor based on *teamwork*, not *surveillance*.

Also consider the "tone at the top" of your company and the messages that are being sent to employees related to cybersecurity practices. Encourage senior management to cultivate an environment where everyone has shared responsibility for cybersecurity. Ideally, employees should have a direct line of communication with someone in the company's chief information security officer's (CISO's) department and understand they can reach out to that person for judgment and hassle-free guidance.

It's also crucial that company management invests in quality employee training related to cybersecurity. It's now considered a best practice that employees receive a general security awareness training, which may focus largely or exclusively on cybersecurity. Also, training should not be a "one-and-done" exercise. The CISO's department or the GC should regularly provide updates to employees via email on recent developments in cybersecurity and other issues they should be aware of. This is the kind of constant reinforcement that cultivates a true culture of CyberWellness℠.

A good place to start in evaluating a company's cybersecurity culture is to review the company's written and formal guidance on the use and protection of company systems. For example, does the company have a written policy regarding employees' use of personal email to conduct company business? How is that policy implemented and observed? Does the board abide by the same standard, or are exceptions made? Ideally, directors will be able to lead by example. Understand that as a director, you may be a particularly attractive target for a cyber breach, as it's known that directors often use personal devices to download board books and communicate about sensitive, nonpublic company information.

In all, an excellent CyRM^{SM} program needs to become a strategic focus embedded in the day-to-day operations and core values of the company. The new paradigm should be that cybersecurity is an ongoing risk that needs to be managed by everyone in the organization.

When employees (of your company or of other companies) make missteps on this front, use these experiences as textbook examples of what not to repeat—anywhere in the firm. Because breaches often result in legal action, the board should include lawyers in their discussions and make sure their efforts to change corporate culture are seasoned with a legal perspective. After assuring that the tone at the top is one of integrity and effective compliance, the board should turn to strategic considerations.

The board should participate in selecting key personnel, such as the CISO. They should also ensure that adequate systems are in place to monitor those individuals' performances. In times past, companies often delegated responsibility for cybersecurity to the company's chief operations officer or chief technology officer. Consider the officer who currently has primary responsibility for cybersecurity at your company. Is that person C-suite level? Is cybersecurity only one of many, pressing demands that person is currently juggling? If the answer to the first question is "no," and the second "yes," you may want to consider creating a new role in the form of a CISO.

The board should also consider the internal reporting structure for the CISO (or other officer with primary responsibility for cybersecurity) to ensure this individual has the independence and authority needed to succeed in this mission-critical role. The CISO may report to the company's chief information officer, chief risk officer, chief operations officer, chief technology officer, or even the chief executive officer—but in any case, the CISO should have access to senior management and the board as needed. Company management should also consider establishing an information security committee chaired by the company's CISO, and invite C-suite officers to attend the committee's meetings. Directors, for their part, should understand who fills the CISO role and engage directly with that individual as appropriate.

From the board's perspective, the key to effective oversight is to hold senior management responsible for articulating and monitoring the company's strategy and risk tolerance related to cybersecurity.

In most cases, board members should have their noses, but not their fingers, in the company's cybersecurity program.

One area where boards can, and should, play a crucial role is in developing the company's strategic plan related to cybersecurity. Following this initial effort, the board should oversee company management in implementing the strategic plan.

The board should also work with management to develop a cyber incident "response playbook" mapping out how the company would respond to various contingencies in the event of a breach or serious cyber incident impacting company systems. For example, in the wake of the Uber scandal, a company may want to consider how it would approach a ransom request, weighing the pros of potentially mitigating some of the damage associated with a breach against the cons of rewarding criminal behavior in this manner. Any such analysis should be flexible enough to take into account of-the-moment law enforcement recommendations and a legal analysis of the company's disclosure obligations. To avoid an Equifax problem, the public response plan should designate an internal and external team of professionals to investigate the causes and make appropriate disclosures.

There are various frameworks that company management can use to develop appropriate risk management strategies related to cybersecurity. For example, in October 2013, the US Department of Commerce's National Institute of Standards and Technology (NIST) issued for comment a set of voluntary standards and best practices for reducing cybersecurity risk. The final version was released in February 2014, titled "Framework for Improving Critical Infrastructure Cybersecurity."

The NIST framework includes five "functional areas," which directors may consider in developing an overarching cybersecurity plan for their companies. These functions include:

Identify: Develop the organizational understanding to manage cybersecurity risk to systems, assets, data, and capabilities.
Protect: Develop and implement the appropriate safeguards to ensure delivery of critical infrastructure services.
Detect: Develop and implement the appropriate activities to identify the occurrence of a cybersecurity event.
Respond: Develop and implement the appropriate activities to take action regarding a detected cybersecurity event.

Recover: Develop and implement the appropriate activities to maintain plans for resilience and to restore any capabilities or services that were impaired due to a cybersecurity event.

Guidelines from the SEC also provide valuable assistance to directors, given the agency's considerable influence in markets. Cybersecurity has long been a priority of the SEC's National Exam Program, which is overseen by the Office of Compliance Inspections and Examinations (OCIE). In August 2017, OCIE posted a risk alert highlighting the results of its Cybersecurity 2 Initiative. Although this initiative focuses only on broker dealers, investment advisers, and funds—entities over which the SEC has primary jurisdiction—the findings of OCIE provide a template that directors of companies in other industries and their management can use to evaluate their own efforts in cybersecurity. As part of the Cybersecurity 2 Initiative, OCIE assessed how companies managed their cybersecurity programs in the following areas:

   i Governance and risk assessment
   ii Access rights and controls
   iii Data loss prevention
   iv Vendor management
   v Training
   vi Incident response

From a broad perspective, OCIE found that while firms were doing more to establish cybersecurity programs, they weren't doing enough to maintain and update those programs in light of the constantly changing cyberthreats and attacks. For example, OCIE noted that nearly all firms had plans that address access incidents, such as denial of service incidents and unauthorized intrusions; however, less than two–thirds of advisers and funds surveyed appeared to adequately maintain such plans.

Directors should approach monitoring their companies' cybersecurity efforts like ongoing maintenance of machinery. Regular checks and adjustments will be needed, and it isn't a one-time exercise. Technical means for conducting and preventing cyberattacks will constantly evolve. Moreover, old tactics and systems may be deemed irrelevant or insufficient as the company moves toward different operating systems or expands its business portfolio.

Accordingly, it's wise for directors to have a standing review of the company's cybersecurity program at quarterly meetings, at the very least. There should also be a procedure in place for briefing the board more frequently if new and serious issues emerge. The company's board minutes should accurately reflect when cybersecurity is discussed at such meetings so that the board's diligence is documented and demonstrated. Boards should also regularly receive a cybersecurity scorecard that highlights the company's progress mitigating cyber risk, including external metrics, gap remediation, emerging risks, trade-offs, and other issues. The scorecard doesn't need to include highly technical key performance indicators to be effective. Instead, examples of good metrics for the board include: customer satisfaction (customer system downtime caused by information security incidents); reputation (number of information security incidents reported in the media); and financials (information security budget as a percent of IT budget).

As an important principle, boards should ensure that management and company employees collect, analyze, and share data regarding cybersecurity incidents—both large and small—to help inform the effectiveness of ongoing cybersecurity efforts. The company should also prioritize collecting, analyzing, and sharing internally any information the company may receive from government, private, or nonprofit sources regarding cyber vulnerabilities and possible exposure.

Following Equifax, it's important for all companies to take a hard look at their information escalation protocols. Who's informed when a possible cyber incident is first picked up on the company's radar? Oftentimes, more junior employees will be best-placed to observe the first signs of a cyber breach. When it comes to installing critical software patches—such as in Equifax's case—ensure there are systems in place for appropriate supervision and peer review so that one person's human error doesn't result in a catastrophic (and preventable) breach.

Directors should also ensure the company has a system in place to encourage employees and management to learn from past mistakes. Acknowledging mistakes and learning from them leads to better decision-making. Cybersecurity postmortems should be encouraged in briefings about the company's security model and vulnerabilities.

When a mistake occurs, this is also a good time to consult a lawyer. Certain mistakes come with legal responsibilities. For example, a company may have to disclose cybersecurity risks and adverse cyber events to its shareholders. Boards should make sure any postmortem, and any policy that grows out of it, includes the necessary legal response.

More and more public companies are describing cybersecurity as a risk in their financial disclosures each year. But what to disclose, and when to disclose it, remains a thorny issue for many. Equifax received significant criticism for waiting until September to disclose a breach it discovered in late July. But companies and regulators alike are realizing that there's a major tension between disclosing early and waiting to learn all material facts in order to avoid making misleading or inaccurate disclosures. The SEC itself was subject to criticism for its perceived missteps in handling the EDGAR data breach. The SEC first reported that no personally identifying information was taken; it later had to revise those statements. Also, the breach happened in 2016, but it was reported to the public in September 2017.

It's critically important for companies to have appropriate escalation protocols in place. Don't lose precious time waiting for the report of a breach to slowly make its way up the chain to decision-makers. Instead, any time between a material breach and disclosure should be well spent investigating the facts and analyzing the issues.

The SEC has provided some guidance in this area. In 2011, the SEC's Division of Corporation Finance published guidance for public companies concerning disclosure obligations related to cybersecurity threats and adverse cyber events. The guidance recommends that material information regarding cyber risk and adverse cyber events should be disclosed if necessary to make other disclosures not misleading. In particular, a company should review its cyber risks in light of the severity and frequency of prior cyber events. Companies should also consider the adequacy of their cyber defenses in light of the risks present in their particular industry. Companies should avoid generic risk factor disclosure and instead should consider their unique facts and circumstances. For example, a disclosure that a threat *may* occur may be insufficient if a company has *already* experienced that threat. A company should also consider including a discussion of cyber risks and incidents in the management discussion and analysis (MD&A)

portion of its regular filings if the costs or consequences associated with the cyber risk or incident are likely to have a material effect on the company's financial condition.

While the SEC has yet to dip its toe, other regulators have already been active in enforcing cyber-related disclosure obligations. For example, in August 2017, Uber settled charges brought by the Federal Trade Commission (FTC) relating to a 2014 breach. The FTC alleged that the company made deceptive claims about its efforts to safeguard customer information and failed to undertake "reasonable, low-cost measures" to prevent unauthorized access to customers' personal data. Meanwhile, the FTC has confirmed that it is currently scrutinizing Uber's response to the 2016 breach, which the company only recently disclosed.

The FTC also previously brought a case against Oracle for disclosure issues, claiming that the company failed to inform consumers that newer software updates wouldn't automatically remove older (and potentially exploitable) versions of Oracle's Java software. Last year the Consumer Financial Protection Bureau (CFPB) ordered Dwolla Inc., a company that operates an online payment system, to pay a penalty and improve its security practices after the company allegedly misrepresented to consumers that its networks were "safe" and "secure," and that its data security practices "exceeded" or "surpassed" industry security standards.

Additionally, while there's no national "data breach notification" law as of yet, the vast majority of states have enacted laws that require entities to notify affected individuals in the event of certain cybersecurity breaches involving sensitive consumer and personally identifiable information.

Uber may well be the most egregious example of delayed disclosure and "what not to do." The company failed to notify regulators and individuals affected by the breach for nearly a year, possibly in violation of state notification laws. Moreover, Uber allegedly made nondisclosure of the breach a condition of its ransom payment to the cybercriminals, only further perpetuating the image of a cover-up. Several states' attorneys general have already initiated investigations into the breach.

The key takeaway is that it's absolutely essential for companies to review the adequacy and timeliness of their cyber disclosures on an ongoing basis. There's no "one-size-fits-all" answer. The advice of experienced disclosure counsel is crucial.

If recent events have taught us anything, it's that a company's cybersecurity protocols are all for naught if the company fails to ensure that third-party service providers also implement adequate cyber risk management systems. All too often, the entry point for the cybercriminals is a third party that has access to the company's systems or nonpublic data.

Home Depot, for example, is still feeling the reverberations from a 2014 cyber incident in which hackers took advantage of a security flaw in a third-party payment processor to steal email and payment information of more than 50 million Home Depot customers. Hackers similarly used a third-party vendor to access Target's customer database in 2013 and stole payment information from approximately 40 million customers.

The example of Deloitte demonstrates why companies should pay attention to professional service firms in particular when it comes to third-party cyber risk. Professional service firms—such as law firms, auditors, and consultants—are particularly vulnerable because their databases and cloud computing applications often contain sensitive information from many different clients and business partners, all in one convenient location for cybercriminals to exploit. The information that professional service firms possess is an appealing target for cybercriminals because it's relatively easy to monetize through illegal trading. Such information may also be an attractive target for hacktivists.

The 2016 "Panama Papers" scandal was one of the first major incidents to shed light on law firm cyber vulnerabilities. The compromised firm, Mossack Fonseca, had helped hundreds of US clients establish offshore businesses. The hack compromised the sensitive information of Mossack Fonseca's high-profile clients, dating as far back as the 1970s, and left many companies that had worked with the firm exposed. We saw a similar set of circumstances unfold in the "Paradise Papers" scandal involving the release of confidential client information from the Appleby law firm.

Because third parties often have access to highly sensitive company information, they should be subject to a rigorous third-party cyber risk assessment before companies engage them. Directors don't need to be aware of the nitty-gritty details of each and every contract for services, but they should ensure that the company has a written vendor risk management policy in place for addressing third parties' access to company systems and sensitive nonpublic data. At the very least, the policy should ensure that management conducts proper due diligence and is aware of the risks of doing business with particular vendors. The company should also routinely reassess third-party risk and ensure that third-party service providers are in fact complying with their obligations.

Boards should also be aware of the risks associated with providing the government with sensitive nonpublic information. The breach of the SEC's EDGAR database raises serious questions about how much sensitive company data should be held by market regulators and whether the government, with its limited resources, can protect such data. When possible, companies should consider providing information on encrypted physical media versus through secure file transfer.

Cybersecurity isn't a problem to be solved—it's an ongoing risk to be managed and, where prudent, transferred. As part of a company's risk management effort, its board should carefully review existing contracts with third-party vendors and insurance policies. These agreements must clearly state who's liable and what's covered in case of a breach.

Although cyber insurance is still in its nascent stages, with little actuarial data, it's one of the fastest growing types of coverage among US companies—and with good reason. The costs associated with a cyberattack can be game-changing for a company. A recent study conducted by Ponemon Institute shows that the average cost globally of a data breach is $3.62 million. Victims of large-scale cyberattacks could expect to add several zeros to that figure, as damage to reputation, costs of notification, and protracted litigation quickly add up.

In its annual report filed with the SEC earlier this year, Target Corporation reported that it had incurred $292 million in cumulative expenses in connection with the 2013 data breach of its systems, which resulted in the massive theft of customers' credit card information.

According to the company, this total amount was offset, in part, by $90 million in insurance payments. Similarly, in 2017, FedEx's Dutch subsidiary was hit by the "NotPetya" virus, which caused a temporary shutdown in the company's operations and led to a $300 million hit to its quarterly profit. FedEx didn't have insurance coverage for the attack, and FedEx's chief financial officer has since revealed that the incident triggered an internal reevaluation as to whether the company should purchase cyber insurance moving forward.

In addition to the obvious potential benefit of a monetary insurance recovery, seeking cyber insurance may result in ancillary advantages for companies. A company that's in the market for cyber insurance will be incentivized to use best practices, as premiums will be based, at least to some extent, on the company's effective use of protective measures. The application process alone may require an in-depth evaluation of a company's existing cyber program. Through this process, the company may gain a better appreciation of its own cyber risks and opportunities. Boards should also be aware that insurance carriers often offer tools to help companies respond to cybersecurity incidents and mitigate post-breach losses, should the need arise.

Boards are commonly in a position to have the final say on whether a company should purchase cyber insurance. Making this decision as a board may require navigating some new terrain. You must determine what is (and should be) covered, and what is not (and need not be) covered. You also need to determine whether a particular premium is fair. One question boards should ask is whether existing insurance policies may cover certain events. Traditionally, most commercial general liability (CGL) policies didn't contain cyber "exclusions"; however, these days, insurers may be more likely to include such provisions in their policies. Directors should ensure there are no critical gaps in coverage and consider what coverage makes the most sense based on their company's own risk profile—for example, coverage options may include coverage for costs of data breaches; extortion; forensic analyses; theft; litigation costs and expenses; and business interruption, to name a few. Boards should also confirm that their directors and officers (D&O) policies include coverage of cybersecurity-related events.

There's nothing stagnant about cybersecurity. The hacks are ever evolving, and defensive practices that are industry standard one month may be obsolete the next. Legislators and regulators, in turn, strive to keep pace with new laws and regulations, spurred in no small part by public outcry following high-profile breaches. The state of New York, for example, responded to the Equifax breach by proposing regulation to expand the state's first-of-its-kind cybersecurity rules, which currently require all financial institutions in New York to register with the state and implement programs to protect consumer data, among other things. The new regulation would extend the requirements to credit reporting agencies. New York's attorney general also proposed new legislation to amend the state's existing data breach notification law. Notably, the proposed legislation would expand the definition of "private information" and apply to any entity that holds the private information of New Yorkers, even if that entity doesn't conduct regular business in the state.

The shifting legal landscape governing cybersecurity may itself be considered a cyber "vulnerability" for a company. Boards need to be cognizant of their companies' compliance obligations, but that's easier said than done. Companies today operate in a fragmented system of cybersecurity regulations. State, federal, and foreign regulators all come with their own rules and guidance. Certain states, such as California and New York, have taken a particularly aggressive tack in recent years to regulate and enforce cybersecurity standards within their jurisdictional limits. On the federal level, agencies such as the FTC and SEC are on the vanguard of cybersecurity enforcement within their own designated areas of focus and guidance. The European Union, for its part, implemented its General Data Protection Regulation, which imposes reporting and other requirements on companies that collect credit card data or other personal information from EU citizens.

Boards should ensure their companies continue to comply with the latest array of state and federal laws and regulations concerning cybersecurity. This is especially true for companies in certain industries that are frequently targeted by cybercriminals (e.g., financial institutions), and for those that handle sensitive personal information, such as personally identifiable information, financial information, or protected health information, as these companies are often subject to scrutiny by regulators and legislators. One obvious first step for the board may be to ask the company's general counsel and CISO to brief the board regularly on legislative developments and provide their recommendations. With many law firms growing their data privacy and cybersecurity practices, companies can also draw on the expertise of outside counsel to develop individualized programs to manage cybersecurity risk, in view of the company's needs.

Boards can also be valuable weapons in combating "compliance fatigue," in which personnel performing the day-to-day compliance functions lose sight of the broader picture as they navigate disparate, daily demands and multiple moving targets. It's important to "check the boxes," but that isn't enough. With their high-level perspective and status, boards can play a major role in encouraging management to think critically and innovatively when it comes to improving existing processes and cybersecurity measures. In the end, boards should try to ensure that the lion's share of the company's effort is spent on actual cybersecurity, not on merely demonstrating compliance.

CyRM℠ ACTION POINTS:
RESPONSIBILITIES OF SENIOR EXECUTIVES
AND BOARD MEMBERS

- Evaluate effectiveness of internal systems and controls.
- Participate in selecting key cybersecurity personnel.
- Make sure cybersecurity personnel have board access.
- Understand and develop metrics for evaluating cybersecurity effectiveness. Take a hard look at escalation protocols. Request a security scorecard.
- Develop an incident response plan. Test the plan. Consider simulated cyberattacks.
- Put mitigating controls in place for third-party contracts.
- Review cyber insurance coverage.
- Have a public response plan in place should a catastrophic cyberattack occur.
- Carefully consider when and how the company will disclose a breach.
- Regularly reassess your cyber plan in light of the shifting legal landscape.
- Initiate a standing review of your cyber program on at least a quarterly basis.
- Task general counsel and/or the CISO with briefing the board on regulatory developments. Leverage preexisting relationships with outside counsel.

PRONG 2
CYBERWELLNESS^{SM}

6

CYBERWELLNESS^{SM}

A Companywide Approach

It's impossible to centrally control every connection with employees and clients—therefore, a new paradigm is required. A company's CyRM^{SM} program needs to encompass not only the firm as a whole, but every employee. Everyone in the company is responsible for the risks they undertake. This requires an active process—just like physical wellness programs in which the company takes an active approach to promoting and maintaining employees' good health. So, too, with CyberWellness^{SM}: proactive choices need to be made across multiple dimensions of cyber defense, response, and governance.

As you've seen in earlier chapters, the traditional approach to cybersecurity relies on prevention strategies. This outmoded approach assumes there's a hardened shell surrounding your firm's IT system. It wrongly assumes that cybersecurity incidents are exceptions—the rare piercing of the hardened shell—rather than frequent, ongoing, and ever-more-creative attempts at breaching data. Good CyRM^{SM} programs say: enough of the old way, it's time to practice comprehensive CyberWellness^{SM}.

The key to effective CyberWellness^{SM} is your company's ability to assess, measure, monitor, and control risk. Most companies generally focus on breaches, which is really only the assessment aspect. They need to broaden their focus, develop new measures like cyber risk tolerances, develop innovative monitoring techniques as key performance indicators, provide cybersecurity training to employees, and implement better cyber-related controls that are incorporated into updated policies and procedures.

To continue the wellness analogy, consider that in recent years, we've seen our public health systems try to shift from reactive mode to proactive—focusing on preventing illness rather than just responding to disease outbreaks when they happen. (The COVID-19 pandemic has heightened our understanding that simply being reactive doesn't work well!)

In contrast to treating incidents as rare exceptions, an intelligence-driven mindset assumes that the company has already been compromised and therefore needs to continuously evolve to stay ahead of the curve. For instance, at my hillside house, I have multiple layers of security. There's a wrought-iron fence around the perimeter of the yard, signs that read "Beware of Dog" and "Protected by Post Alarm," light-sensitive floodlights, an alarm system that's wired to every door and window, a fireproof safe hidden well out of sight, and a panic button next to my bed. My goal is to deter bad actors with my fence, my floodlights, and the signs on my fence. But if they should decide to break in anyway, then I have multiple layers of defense in place: doors, windows, and screens alarmed, internal beams should the bad guys somehow manage to get in without setting off an external alarm, the panic button, a big dog with a big bark, and the hidden safe. It's not enough to rely on the exterior security measures. You may think that's excessive, but when you're an expert in risk management, you know it's better to be safe than sorry.

My approach to home safety—which is an analog version of a dynamic CyRMˢᴹ program—succeeds because it's comprehensive. One way to consider preparing for cyberattacks is an approach called "Defense in Depth." This approach is modeled after conventional military strategy. Rather than concentrating all resources at the front line, the "Defense in Depth" strategy has defenders deployed in a series of preplanned positions—a series of layers—from which they can advantageously attack the advancing enemy. Adapted to cybersecurity, "Defense in Depth" strategies use multiple security techniques and products to mitigate the potential failure of one component. "Defense in Depth" also slows down the attacker and buys time to fix the problem.

When serial bank robber Willie Sutton was asked why he felt compelled to rip off financial institutions, he replied, "That's where the money is." The same goes for cybercriminals. Your firm needs to decide which data is the most valuable and then spend accordingly to protect it. For example, confidential client information (social security numbers, say) may be the most critical and should receive the most protection. If that's the case, allocate a large share of your cybersecurity budget toward client information protection.

When thinking about protecting client data, keep in mind that it's no longer simply a question of having data stolen—there's also the concern that the data will be altered to make it unusable or incorrect. This is something criminals do under the nose of a firm, and it can take ages to come to light! It's therefore critical that your company puts in place the most effective strategy or strategies to protect important data. Once you've ascertained the criticality of what needs to be protected, you can prioritize and allocate resources to avoid and mitigate cybersecurity threats. At that point, you can decide whether or not your cybersecurity budget is appropriate.

It's also important to have a comprehensive command of the terms and conditions of other risk-mitigating items—such as insurance—with the corresponding knowledge of where insurance and other risk mitigation efforts won't be effective. For example, your company is a trusted adviser to your clients. If your company experiences a cyberattack and as a result loses your top clients' highly personal financial data, that could be enough of a reputational hit to put your firm out of business.

Smart companies understand that CyberWellness℠ isn't a technical problem to be solved, but rather an ongoing risk to be managed. Cybersecurity cannot be guaranteed, but a timely and appropriate reaction can. With that in mind, let's consider the best way to prepare for being hacked.

Incident Response Plans

Your company should create incident response plans that consider both public relations and legal issues. An incident response plan helps to identify, respond to, and recover from cybersecurity incidents. The objective of an incident response plan is to prevent damages such as service outages, data loss, or theft, as well as to illicit access to organizational systems.

An incident response plan isn't complete without a team that can carry it out. Team members are the point people for the incident—they're responsible for communicating with internal partners and external parties, such as legal counsel, press, law enforcement, customers, and other stakeholders. In order for the incident response team to be effective, they need senior management support, consistent testing, and clear communication channels. The team needs to develop a response plan that provides a structured process for each of these steps:

- **Preparation:** Perform a risk assessment and prioritize security issues. Identify which are the most sensitive assets and, by extension, which are the critical security incidents the team should focus on to contain the issue. Create a communication plan and prepare documentation that clearly and briefly outlines roles, responsibilities, and processes.
- **Identification:** When a potential incident is discovered, the team should immediately collect additional evidence, decide on the type and severity of the incident, and document everything they're doing.
- **Containment:** Once the team identifies a security incident, the immediate goal is to contain the incident and prevent further damage.
- **Eradication:** The team must identify the root cause of the attack and take steps to prevent similar ones in the future. For example, if a vulnerability was exploited, it should be immediately patched.
- **Recovery:** The team should bring affected production systems back online carefully to ensure another incident doesn't take place, then test and verify that affected systems are back to normal.
- **Documentation of lessons learned:** Investigate the incident further to identify if it could happen again, then take necessary steps to ensure it won't.

Penetration Testing

A healthy CyberWellnessˢᴹ program also practices *penetration testing*—also known as pen testing. Pen testing views your network, application, device, and physical security through the eyes of both a malicious actor and an experienced cybersecurity expert to discover weaknesses and identify areas where your security posture needs improvement. Pen testing doesn't stop at just discovering ways in which a criminal might gain unauthorized access to sensitive data, or even take over your systems for malicious purposes. It also simulates a real-world attack to determine how your defenses will fare, and the possible magnitude of a breach. Such evaluations (perhaps performed by an independent third party) provide insight into your organization's overall cyber resilience, which is a continuously evolving objective.

Pen testing isn't just about what's wrong. It's also about identifying appropriate trade-offs—because you can't protect everything. Comprehensive penetration testing considers several areas: application, networks (including wireless), weak passwords and protocols, and physical barriers, such as sensors and cameras.

Just as you go to a health care provider for an annual wellness checkup, it makes sense to enlist the help of highly trained security consultants to carry out your security testing. While you might think you're perfectly healthy, a doctor can run tests to detect dangers you're not aware of. Similarly, the people who put together, maintain, and monitor your security program may not have the objectivity needed to identify security flaws, understand the level of risk for your organization, and help address and fix critical issues. Metaphorically speaking, in this ongoing game of cat and mouse, you would be smart to consult with an objective outside cat every so often because the mice are fast and sneaky—always learning, always evolving, inventing new ways to steal your cheese.

Tabletop Exercises

Tabletop exercises help determine how your team will react to a potential cyberattack so you can evaluate the effectiveness of your planning. Companies can identify flaws or gaps in their response and make adjustments to ensure top-notch preparedness. For instance, if your company experienced a ransomware attack, would your employees know what to do? Testing this scenario in a safe environment lets you know if your response plan for ransomware is effective and whether it can be improved using other alternatives. Tabletop exercises can also help you identify missing links in the chain of command—ensuring documentation of response plans and finding gaps in your recovery process. An excellent outside eye can identify and develop tabletop exercises that will help your company strengthen its security and resiliency.

Public Relations and Legal Counsel

An important component of cyber resilience entails having external experts and firms on board to support a decisive, effective response to any data breach. The post-breach environment isn't the time to be searching for required expertise or negotiating contractual terms, so having a team of external pros on board can speed recovery and resumption of operations. These external experts should specialize in forensics, legalities, communications, and systems remediation, among others. Your approach to law enforcement (FBI and others) should also be considered in advance of an incident.

Repeat after me: cybersecurity cannot be guaranteed, but a timely and appropriate reaction can.

Establish Effective Governance

Companies need an effective governance structure to ensure that staff and everyone you work with can conduct accurate, timely assessments to identify current and emerging vulnerabilities. It's best to use an outside professional to review your governance structure. It's critical to involve professionals with the appropriate technical skills and knowledge of the current risk environment. A tech-oriented professional versed in the cyber world can be an indispensable resource.

Ongoing Workforce Training and Development

Research indicates that two-thirds of successful cyberattacks are directly attributable to the actions (or inactions) of employees. Companies must ensure that employees understand the wide variety and ever-changing nature of cyberthreats. They need to know how their own actions can help safeguard company assets. Therefore, improving awareness of employees to risk exposures is critical in strengthening your organization's overall cyber resilience. Any measurable improvement in employee awareness—through initiatives such as gamification and ongoing training that's operational in nature—would be highly accretive to your organization's capacity to protect and respond to a cyber incident.

Unfortunately, most employees aren't interested in their own personal digital security, much less their company's. Historically, anything having to do with IT security was kept away from users by IT teams. Is it any wonder, then, that users show little to no interest in their company's cybersecurity? Undoing that disinterest is hard. Changing your organization's corporate culture to strengthen cybersecurity is very difficult. It requires a paradigm shift to CyberWellness℠ that keeps pace with evolving cyberthreats.

If you think about it, users and employees should be the front line of data security. After all, they're the ones who create and handle information. They're in the best position to understand its value. Senior management should implement interactive training and accountability programs that *engage* with users and employees. Modern game-based training—with follow-up monitoring to see how users and employees apply their training—can transform a company's culture into one where cybersecurity is everyone's job. It's important to cultivate and nurture a continuous learning environment—including relevant and memorable training and tools to support strong cyber hygiene, ranging from password protocols to antiphishing campaigns to "bring your own device" policies.

In addition, it's essential you create a safe environment in which users and employees at all levels are encouraged to point out weaknesses and vulnerabilities without worry that the messenger will be killed. Users and employees need to know they're acknowledged and rewarded when they identify an unmitigated risk or emerging threat. You want them to bring you "bad news," because you can't prevent or fix vulnerabilities if you don't know they exist. A healthy CyberWellness℠ culture praises and thanks the messengers—it doesn't kill them.

Implement Management Processes for All Third-Party Vendors and Suppliers

Third parties can be positively impactful to an operating environment. However, companies aren't usually as attuned to cybersecurity risks from third parties as they are for their own businesses.

They should be! Third parties can create the same adverse, long-term effects as company employees. Consider that the sharing of data and communication between your company and its vendors is no longer fully in control of the internal operations of your company. Vendors and suppliers are external parties that create new entry points into a company's technology environment, adding complexity and potential volatility to the operating environment.

Here are some basic ground rules for any healthy third-party program:

- Prioritize third-party exposures based on risk (including cyber) to the organization.
- Put clear assessment tools in place for the onboarding of any new relationships.
- Implement ongoing, risk-adjusted monitoring processes to assess adherence to contract terms and joint disaster recovery testing with primary service providers.

Legal and other practical considerations can (and should) be employed to partition and mitigate the risk introduced through third-party relationships. Risk—no matter where it originates—will rebound to your company in times of crisis or stress. Clients and customers, both corporate and individual, will always look to *your* company for explanations and relief when problems occur. Try explaining to someone who's had their Social Security number compromised that the problem came from a B2B vendor.

Take a Step Back

While I've touched on several different steps your company needs to make to have a healthy and resilient cybersecurity program in place, I want to reiterate that feeling reasonably secure about your company's cybersecurity program isn't just a matter of being able to answer questions like: "Does our organization have the right governance structure?" Rather, it's being able to answer bigger questions, such as: "Are we thinking about security the right way, and where is all this going?" By being proactive in your approach to CyberWellnessˢᴹ, you'll keep yourself, your clients, and your employees as safe as possible.

CyRM℠ ACTION POINTS: CYBERWELLNESS

- Make proactive choices across multiple dimensions of cyber defense, response, and governance.
- Understand that it's not simply a question of what could go wrong today, but also what else can happen tomorrow.
- Appreciate that there are no offensive strategies in cybersecurity—only defensive ones.
- Put in place security incident response plans that consider both public relations and legal issues.
- Develop strong, detailed policies backed with ongoing workforce training and development.
- Implement management processes for all third-party vendors and suppliers.

7

CULTIVATE A STRONG CULTURE TO ENHANCE CYBERSECURITY

We all know that corporate cultures don't change quickly—they migrate. Most organizational development experts offer the same recipe for culture change:

1. Pick the right leadership.
2. Recognize and reward the behaviors you want to encourage.
3. Communicate clear values.
4. Provide extensive training.

This recipe won't work for the ever-evolving, shape-shifting, constantly moving target that is cybersecurity. Most employees aren't interested in their own digital security, much less their company's. Therefore, changing a company's culture to strengthen security is especially difficult, requiring a paradigm shift to keep pace with the threat landscape.

Most people think of security as the protection of a company's digital environment—a virtual hardened shell, protected by security guarding the company's networks, servers, and applications. The problem with this paradigm is that when you focus on the environment, the security employed becomes an end in itself and isn't directly related to the data it's trying to protect.

For example, suppose a company is trying to defend against data loss or the unauthorized use of data. Isn't it far better, from a security perspective, if the data itself are not readily readable and can be tracked based on those with authorized access and the business context in which it's being used?

Further, this approach still works through the multiple defensive layers that a company may implement as part of a "Defense in Depth" strategy.

Data-Centric Security

When we shift our focus from the IT infrastructure to the data that need to be protected, the first step is defining what the crucial data are. Once that's defined, you can use new, proven solutions to control how the data are handled and distributed.

Encryption, for example, can help ensure that data are secure whether at rest or in motion. But it isn't fail-safe, because once cybercriminals intrude into a network with stolen, valid user credentials, encryption becomes useless.

Data masking, which is the process of hiding specific data, is another useful tool. Data masking can be achieved a number of ways: by obscuring the data dynamically as users perform requests; duplicating data to eliminate the subset of the data that need to be hidden; or just masking the data from users or third parties.

Another way to control data is through the use of data loss prevention (DLP) solutions, which can provide accurate information regarding the movement of sensitive data—and even block the transfer or delete it when found on unauthorized endpoints. Ongoing monitoring of the data using DLP solutions can help identify breaches in a timely fashion and limit the damage inflicted. The paradigm shift—focusing on the security of the data employing data-centric security—will change your corporate culture. Here's how you can do it.

Get the Users Involved

Historically, anything to do with IT security was kept away from users by IT teams. Little wonder that users show little or no interest in the company's security.

In reality, users are the front line of data security. They create and handle the data and are best placed to understand the value of the data. Case in point: Allianz Ireland forced its users to select a data classification before a document could be shared or an email sent. The company experienced a rapid culture change within just a few months, resulting in a 60% increase in employee awareness of data security practices and an 89% reduction of breaches.

Engage Employees in Training Applications

Today's cyber risk training focuses on phishing schemes, not protecting data. Most training programs aren't engaging, interesting, or fun. They try to teach with borderline yes/no questions, and usually 80% of them have "yes" for an answer. No one fails as long as they answer all the questions. Borrrring! Now suppose the cybersecurity training is a video game, and you're having fun role-playing a bad guy who stole valid user credentials and is now trying to steal company data. You receive points based on how far you go in successfully stealing data.

The game is highly engaging, and at the end of the session you obtain a point score that, if high enough, comes with a reward. Even better, the company now has valid data to determine employees' cyber awareness—information that could be used to help purchase cyber insurance.

Make Diversity Part of the Security Culture

Self-awareness and consciousness are the first steps toward changing any undesired behavior or attitude. Employees' decision-making related to security is influenced by their diversity, their background, openness to discussing these issues, and attitude about community. But posters, screen savers, and even in-person group reviews will barely influence your employees' ability to judge threats.

Suppose a data breach occurs and it's used as a learning experience for everyone. Instead of just creating a PowerPoint, why not have employees try to write a phishing email for the company? This approach takes into account the diversity of your employees and their varying levels of understanding of the threat.

Long term, the board needs to understand and consider the strategic business implications of cybersecurity, foster the right corporate culture regarding security, and encourage the integration of cyber risk management practices into all governance and approval processes. Bottom line: a smart board of directors understands that cybersecurity is a management issue, not just a technical one.

CyRM^{SM} ACTION ITEMS: CULTIVATE A STRONG CULTURE

- Assess corporate culture and set the right example.
- C-suite and board members must be more than involved— they should set the tone.
- Training should be engaging.
- Culture should be based on teamwork, not surveillance.

PRONG 3

CYBERSECURITY AS A BUSINESS STRATEGY

8

TRUST WILL BECOME A COMPETITIVE ADVANTAGE

When I started working at Citicorp, business was done on a handshake; your word was considered your bond. Numerous surveys now show that trust among people, businesses, and institutions has declined significantly. It's easy to point to a few main drivers that undermine trust among companies and their customers, suppliers, and employees. Topping the list are large-scale cyberattacks and the development of social media platforms that create immediate transparency. The list also includes countless technological failures like the Google failure that disabled baby monitors and locked people out of their homes.

In our fast-paced, anonymous digital world, information on a company's product is readily available. As one customer service expert puts it, "customers are wired and dangerous." Bad news travels faster than ever before. Being "different" is less and less of a competitive advantage. Instead, customers' trust in your company's credibility is the new coin of the realm—probably *the* most important competitive advantage you can have.

One failure of trust really stands out in my mind. When Samsung's Galaxy Note 7 first hit the review cycle in August 2016, the consensus was "that it might be the best designed smartphone ever." That was before the first phone exploded because the battery had a tendency to simultaneously combust. A month after its release, there'd been reports of at least 35 phones bursting into flames. Samsung issued a humble and apologetic statement in which the company announced it was recalling the Note 7 and issuing replacement devices. OK, except those replacements also began catching fire, including at least one on a plane. TSA banned all Note 7s. You may remember this if you traveled that fall. Eventually, Samsung recalled all the phones and sent out a software update that made existing devices useless. The company's decision to finally own its exploding phones and make good by replacing them with different models was probably what saved the company's reputation. Credit Suisse analysts estimated the damages cost Samsung a cool $17 billion. That's to say nothing of the consumer trust they lost.

Equally important—perhaps even more so—trust includes safeguarding personal data. To gain business, every company must win customers' trust by actually *being* trustworthy. Customers will ask, "Can I trust that cybersecurity is a priority and that my transactions, information, and personal data are correct, secure, and private?" A positive customer experience will be defined as accessible, frictionless, resilient, secure, and transparent.

In the future, trust will become more and more important. Today we live in a world of platforms. We have trust platforms such as Airbnb and eBay that are essentially low-risk environments that encourage strangers to conduct business transactions. We have entertainment platforms like Netflix and iTunes taking trust a step further. If you try to buy an album from iTunes that you already purchased, iTunes will remind you that you already own it. Same with Amazon. Amazon introduced a price-check app, which enables your phone to scan the bar code of any product in any retail store, compare its price with Amazon's, and give you a discount if you buy the item from Amazon.

Not only does the customer have instant access to pricing and the strongest competitors, but the endgame will change. Customers will focus on their relationships with the vendors they buy from (Amazon), not the manufacturers of the products. Trust in an era of transparency, coupled with the power shifting to the consumer, will require companies to place a greater focus on trust and make it a competitive advantage. Trust will define the quality and sustainability of a company's relationship with its various stakeholders.

But trust isn't only for the consumer. Employees' trust will be crucial to foster high levels of collaboration that drive business results. Employees will ask, "Can I trust that my work-related data is secure and private, that networks will function, and that cybersecurity measures are in place?" This will become increasingly important in the new, virtual world, where managing remote teams takes extra effort to make employees feel valued when they're away from headquarters. Trust defines the relationship between companies and suppliers in our interconnected business environment. With data and systems so widely shared, effective data management will become an important differentiator in helping clients succeed with their customers.

Previous dealings and direct relationships will take a back seat to accountability and greater assurances that business partners' governance and compliance processes are aligned with your own. Maintaining trust will build shared values and create a true competitive advantage.

Target's attempt to break into the Canadian market is a lesson in supply chain mismanagement, and how not to move into new markets. The US retailer attempted to open 124 shops and three large distribution centers in the country at the same time. It did this with an apparently faulty computerized-assisted ordering system that left warehouses overflowing with stock while store shelves sat bare. Marc Wulfraat, president of MWPVL International Inc., a logistics and supply chain consulting firm in Montreal, noted that Target "just completely lost control of inventory," something that wouldn't have happened if it had started its entry into Canada with fewer stores and been able to test its distribution network first. The company announced in February 2020 that its travails in the Great White North had lost the firm $1 billion.

We've seen with the COVID-19 pandemic that trust has been expanded to include ecosystem partners. Companies will ask, "Can I trust that measures are being taken to protect my proprietary information and ensure integrity of the transactions, and that service levels are met as business interactions are increasingly virtual?" Even further, trusted companies will try to balance the trust of all their stakeholders. Sandra Sucher a professor at Harvard Business School, notes that "trusted companies know how to balance the trust of all their stakeholders." In one example during the pandemic, a global hotel and resort chain that needed to furlough workers connected its shutdown teams with other companies that needed help in the short term to deal with increased surges in demand.

CyRM^{SM} ACTION POINTS: ON TRUST

- Realize trust will be crucial to foster higher levels of collaboration with employees, consumers, suppliers, and various stakeholders.

9
CYRM℠ AS A VITAL BUSINESS STRATEGY

Today's business world is becoming ever more interconnected. New threats are emerging every day—not just from bad actors, but from the vulnerabilities created by a widening attack surface and enhanced communications. Today, employees can be tracked easily from their mobile phones or fitness watches. Their laptops can be hacked, as well as their cars, watches, TVs, and even their hearing aids! Greater internet connectivity is constantly widening the attack surface. Everything from light bulbs in the office to alarm systems at home to appliances, planes, and pacemakers are vulnerabilities.

Digital communication keeps adding more functionality and control, while at the same time creating new vulnerabilities. Consider, for example, the possibility that your E-ZPass could be used by law enforcement to issue speeding tickets.

Most people assume the main function of CyRM℠ is to reduce operational risk by eliminating the dangers posed by viruses and hackers. But it's time to reposition CyRM℠ for what it really is—*a growth enabler.*

Digital transformation has created an environment of increasingly intense competition. Agile organizations can get the upper hand by using cutting-edge technologies to create new products, provide better customer experiences, innovate, and rapidly scale those innovations across the enterprise. As a result, business strategy and IT strategy will be increasingly and actively more aligned. How a company weaves its technology investments together will ultimately determine how prepared it is to preempt disruption and seize opportunities. Companies that build boundaryless, adaptable, and radically human IT systems that explicitly enable scale and strategic agility will win the day.

To succeed at this, companies will need to reimagine business processes for the future. They (you) need to target multiple processes with the same technologies increasingly dependent on platforms, ecosystems, and large varieties of connected data to fuel artificial intelligence systems. The key enablers for digitization involve cloud, big data, mobility, and collaboration. Security needs to be embedded in the entire business ecosystem—and it needs to be sufficiently agile to adapt to the speeds and volume of data required by daily transactions, all while being able to handle the complexity and multiplicity of threats in a digital world.

Security and governance will become more complicated than today—as more potential attack surfaces increase vulnerability. While developing new products and services, a company needs to strike the right balance between innovation and risk. In most cases, the more that security is increased, the less user-friendly and convenient the product or service becomes. A strong CyRM℠ posture is essential to ensure that innovation isn't curtailed due to security concerns. A sound CyRM℠ strategy must promote innovation as well as customer trust—both essential for continued growth. A well-developed CyRM℠ strategy keeps innovation and the operational wheels of business rolling. Effective CyRM℠ is also needed to enhance product integrity, customer experience, operations, regulatory compliance, brand reputation, and investor confidence.

The business landscape is becoming ever-more interdependent. Business strategies are therefore focused on widening and deepening links to resources outside the firm. Competitive advantage is no longer the sum of all efficiencies, but rather the sum of all connections. Companies need to manage a complex ecosystem of stakeholders: partners, suppliers, investors, and customers. Partners for your network must be selected with governance and fiduciary processes that are aligned with their own. If one link is broken anywhere in the ecosystem, the others will weaken, too, and business will suffer. It's important to adopt CyRM℠ technologies that assess behavior in order to identify potential problems before they can cause harm. Real-time monitoring that enables automated system interventions when anomalous behavior is detected will become the norm.

Companies that embrace these central notions of CyRM℠ and combine them with a "bend but not break" approach that combines cybersecurity, business continuity, and enterprise resilience will gain a competitive advantage. We often are correct in identifying the risks that can harm us, but we usually underestimate their velocity or strength. Companies that elevate the role of security will strengthen customer trust and boost shareholder value.

Two examples of the interconnectedness of CyRMˢᴹ and business strategy come to mind:

> In March 2018 the city of Atlanta was attacked by a ransomware called SamSam. The attack devastated the city government's computer systems, disrupting numerous city services, including police records, courts, utilities, and parking services. Computer systems were shut down for *five days*, forcing many departments to complete essential paperwork by hand. Five days! Think about how aggravated you get when your system is down for five hours. Even though services were slowly brought back online, the full recovery took months.

The attackers demanded a mere $52,000 ransom payment, but when all was said and done, the full impact of the attack was projected to cost more than $17 million. Nearly $3 million alone was spent on contracts for emergency IT consultants and crisis management firms.

The Atlanta ransomware attack is a lesson in inadequate business continuity planning. The event revealed that the city's IT was woefully unprepared for the attack. Just two months earlier, an audit had found 1,500 to 2,000 vulnerabilities in the city's IT systems, which were compounded by "obsolete software and an IT culture driven by ad hoc or undocumented processes."

That was an example of how bad CyRMˢᴹ leads to bad business. Now let's look at a positive example of the interconnectedness. Research shows that 40 percent to 60 percent of small businesses never reopen their doors after a disaster. In August 2017, Hurricane Harvey slammed into Southeast Texas, ravaging homes and businesses across the region. Over the course of four days, some areas received more than forty inches of rain. By the time the storm cleared, it had caused more than $125 billion in damage.

Gaille Media, a small internet marketing agency, refused to be another small company shut down by disaster. Despite being located on the second floor of an office building, Gaille's offices were flooded when Lake Houston overflowed. The flooding was so severe that nobody could enter the building for three months. The company never returned to the building, but its operations were hardly affected. That's because Gaille kept most of its data stored in the cloud, which allowed staff to work remotely through the storm and after. Even with the office destroyed, they never lost access to their critical documents and records. In fact, when it came time to decide where to relocate, the owner ultimately decided to keep the company decentralized, allowing workers to continue working remotely. Had the company kept all its data stored at the office, the business may never have recovered. The COVID-19 pandemic has demonstrated that *the virtual world is already upon us and that the ultimate winners will be the companies that enable it.*

When it comes to corporate crises, the only thing people remember is the outcome. A good outcome is the result of a well-developed, disciplined process that demonstrates collective wisdom and commitment to corrective results.

The specific needs of an effective CyberWellness^{SM} and security program include: careful planning, smart delegation, and a system for monitoring compliance—all of which the board of directors should oversee. Long term, the board needs to understand and consider the strategic business implications of cybersecurity, foster the right corporate culture regarding security, and encourage the integration of CyRM^{SM} practices into all governance and approval processes. Bottom line: a smart board of directors understands that cybersecurity is a management issue—not just as a technical one.

Having an effective business cybersecurity strategy is so important that the SEC will soon mandate it. Now working its way through the Senate, the Cybersecurity Disclosure Act is a simple bill that will have a far-reaching effect. The intent is to ensure that companies publicly disclose the steps they're taking to protect themselves and their customers from cyberattacks.

As part of their annual reporting to the SEC, public companies will have to disclose whether a member of the board "has expertise or experience in cybersecurity." If not, they'll have to be able to cite "what other cybersecurity steps" were taken by the company. Requiring board expertise in information security would be a novelty in corporate America, other than what already exists in companies in the information security business.

More significantly, the Cybersecurity Disclosure Act will hold boards of directors responsible for protecting their companies and their investors from data breaches, hack attacks, and other cyber-threats. This legislation will elevate cybersecurity to the list of other risk factors that public companies must disclose, such as litigation, high debt levels, or labor problems.

In short, to compete and win in today's technology-driven world, companies need to get cybersecurity right.

CyRM^SM ACTION POINTS: ON BUSINESS STRATEGY

- Understand and consider the strategic business implications of cybersecurity.
- Encourage the integration of CyRM^SM into all governance and approval processes.
- Understand that cybersecurity is a managerial issue, not just a technical one.

10
HOW TO THINK ABOUT THE FUTURE

Many years ago, I worked on a strategic plan for Citicorp, during which time I was privileged to spend a day with Peter Drucker, the elder statesmen of management gurus. I asked Drucker how to predict the future, and he replied, "The best way to predict the future is to create it."

Scenario construction and analysis are the perfect tools to predict the future. Scenarios are "what if" stories about the future that allow us to consider almost anything that can happen, both positive and negative, and help us plan various responses. They also involve the creation of boundaries and deciding whether to remain within them. This may remind you of some of the risk management concepts from the previous chapter.

When we build scenarios, we begin by listing the possible drivers of change, then divide them into two broad domains: those things we think we know something about and uncertainties. The former are usually trends that can be extrapolated from the past. We can, for example, make pretty good assumptions about long-term shifts in demographics, based on past and present shifts. Uncertainties include things like interest rates, changes in political power, and as yet unforeseen innovations. Good scenario planning requires a careful blending of known and unknown drivers of change. Once the broad parameters of a scenario are in place, one begins to look for inflection points—or trip wires—that can be monitored to determine whether the events of the day may trigger a chain of events leading toward the fulfillment of the scenario.

A scenario regarding World War III might read as follows:

> In 2021, after a year of increasing tensions between China and the US over the spread of the pandemic, China clamps down

on Hong Kong. The US places steep sanctions on all Chinese exports, causing China's negative growth. Social unrest against the government carries over into the Chinese mainland. International bodies are unable to bring the US and China to the bargaining table. China tries to seize some long-disputed islands in the South China Sea. A brewing crisis steadily escalates over a few incidents, but the tipping point is Taiwan, which declares its independence from China. China subsequently invades Taiwan and launches a ballistic missile volley against a US carrier coming to aid Taiwan. The loss of a major warship and its crew galvanizes the US into action. The US targets Chinese land forces in Taiwan and prevents the reinforcement and resupply of these troops before forcing their surrender. The US simultaneously targets Chinese air and naval units, as well as ships and aircraft held in reserve as the situation escalates. Perhaps you also build out a scenario in which Japan and North Korea begin a conflict.

Even if they're not necessarily predictive, scenarios can challenge our present view of the world, long before events have changed them. In doing so, they provide us with trip wires, and when we stumble across them, much like speed bumps make us aware of our speed, they lead us to consider how we'll be impacted by future events.

In the scenario above, if China was my company's major supplier of component parts, I would obviously be concerned about my alternate supply chains. Perhaps South Korea wouldn't be my first "go-to supplier" if tensions between the US and China escalated. I would also monitor the relationship between Seoul and Tokyo (which has been hostile to date) because in a North Korean intervention, if Seoul and Tokyo both side with the US, the Chinese may spend more time restraining Pyongyang than supporting it in conflict.

When I worked at Citicorp, we monitored the local movement of high-net-worth individuals' capital. Local capital flowing out of an emerging markets country signaled the beginning of problems—best understood, after all, by those in the country—and foretold the eventual devaluation of the country's currency. If we'd waited until local governments acted themselves, instead of monitoring capital flows ourselves, it would already have been too late to react. Not doing anything now about the future often incurs the highest risk. Trip wires allow you to move proactively before events begin to move you.

Making Better Decisions Regarding Risk

Whenever I hear someone say they see "a light at the end of the tunnel," my first thought is that it might be the headlight of an oncoming train. Perhaps a mine shaft is a more appropriate metaphor than a tunnel: we're moving forward in the dark, looking for gold. We can't make decisions about the future based solely on what we see, or what we think we know. In reality, our decisions are always based on incomplete information—it's just the best information we have on hand at the time. As a result, we must learn to manage the risks associated with a decision-making process that's imperfect. We can think of the decision-making process in terms of four steps: assessment of the situation; rules of the game; making the decision; and reevaluating after the fact.

Assessment

It's important to know where you are. A clear-eyed, thorough assessment of your current position is necessary before you can set goals and manage risks. However, the limits of our senses themselves keep us from being aware of much that goes on around us, and this, more often than not, is a good thing. Imagine, for example, if we were able to hear the sounds of the cells in our bodies, endlessly dividing themselves—the roar would deafen us. In fact, it seems as if the ability to think clearly is dependent on a certain level of sensory deprivation. For this reason, most of us avoid noise as we work. In a broader sense, our first sensations at the beginning of every day are our immediate surroundings. Though the process may occur subconsciously, our eyes first take in the familiar sights of our bedrooms, establishing our location. This, it seems, is our mind's way of telling us that in order to know what we're doing, and where we might go, we first have to know where we are. At first, this may appear to be a contradiction—that is, the notion that one can focus both on short-term events and long-term plans—but our lives are full of inconsistencies. The trick lies in knowing how to change your field of vision when the time is right, first studying the details, then stepping back to look at the big picture. Without the details, after all, the big picture doesn't exist at all.

It's equally important to know what you don't know. Understand the limits of your own knowledge and question the assumptions of others. For example, there are numerous studies that predict that the populations of three of the world's five largest economies—the European Union, Japan, and Germany—will decline over the next forty years, as well as those of Italy, Russia, and South Korea. Those changes will unquestionably cause changes in global economic production and will almost certainly tilt the balance of military power. The effects of population aging will greatly exacerbate this trend, reducing the number of productive workers in the world's leading economies, while simultaneously causing the costs of health care to rise. While these assumptions are based on projections—and thus truly on things we don't know—the trends are sufficiently alarming to warrant ongoing examination and questioning of the underlying assumptions in the years to come.

Rules of the Game

It's essential that you determine how much risk you're willing to accept to achieve your goals. What do you have to gain if you achieve your goal? What are you willing to give up to achieve this goal? Years ago, I was engaged by a world-class investment company to help the company's senior management make what we called a "how high is too high" decision. In other words, how much was senior management willing to lose in a given investment position? We went around and around in the CEO's conference room, but we finally settled on the following simple answer: "too high" was a loss that they would be embarrassed to read about on the front page of the *Wall Street Journal*. Staying below that number would give the company's management peace of mind. For them, an appetite for risk was related to a desire to avoid bad publicity. I advised them to put limits on the company's portfolio so that its losses would never exceed the amount they could tolerate seeing on the front page of the newspaper. The company's head of quantitative analysis complained that these limits weren't precise enough. Everyone laughed when I responded: "Better to be approximately right than to be precisely wrong." When you define the rules of the game, it's easier to make decisions.

Making Your Decision

Many years ago, I had lunch with Margaret Thatcher. I asked her, "Prime minister, why did you go to war with Saddam Hussein?" She looked directly into my eyes and said, "You never let a bully push you around. I called up President Bush and we went to war." Her answer taught me that important and difficult decisions should be made based on simple, fundamental principles.

First, and most importantly, we need to identify the risks that we are simply not willing to take, irrespective of any potential personal cost. As COVID-19 took over the world, US Navy Capt. Brett Crozier acted on principle. Faced with the choice between the potential death of hundreds (or thousands) of sailors under his command, versus waiting on the chain of command to act, he chose the safety and well-being of his crew. Likewise, if each of us understands our stress points, we can identify the non-negotiable risks in our own situation that we're simple not willing to take—no matter what. This puts us in a better position to make good decisions earlier in the process.

When evaluating risk, we all tend to *underestimate* the severity and velocity with which those risks can hit. Six months before the 2008 financial crisis, I asked the former CEO of Lehman Brothers, "What's your strategy here?" He answered, "Save Mother!" Does that answer sound vaguely familiar to the answers we hear from others today? It's essential to understand that the best decisions in life are made when you have *real* alternatives. Therefore, take steps now to create realistic contingency plans that will protect you against the downside.

Third, it's important to understand that *risk is the absence of information*. There's risk in everything we do, because we can't possibly know all there is to know—there's always information missing in every situation. Never was that truer than it is with the COVID-19 pandemic. Should you wear a mask or not? How many times a week should you shop for food? How should you be investing your retirement assets in light of this new reality? There are trade-offs with each decision. There's no one-size-fits-all answer for everyone. Risk is personal. I've often said to clients over the years that when everyone is out of work, it's a recession; when you're out of work, it's a depression. You have to do your own personal risk/reward analysis for your daily actions, your financial choices, and choices that affect you, your family, your community—and, indirectly, the whole country.

Making difficult risk decisions is comparable to kissing a rattlesnake. It's never fun and can be fatal. But the more you systematically consider what's really important to you, what information is missing, what the collective wisdom is telling you—and you make a commitment to evaluate "what is my downside relative to what is really important to me"—the better your decisions will be. Though it may be uncomfortable, it's much better to have thoughtfully and carefully evaluated the risks than to not have considered them at all. And if you conclude that you need help to make the right decision, ask for that assistance sooner rather than later. Let the experts help you.

Finally, after a crisis is over, the only thing people will remember are the judgment calls you made and the outcomes you achieved. Nobody will give you credit for good intentions—only final outcomes. The best possible outcome is the result of a thoughtful, disciplined, orderly process that includes collective wisdom and a powerful, laser-focus intention on getting it right.

Reevaluate

Some common sense applies here. Monitor outcomes continuously and learn from your mistakes, so you can make better decisions in the future. The Japanese philosophy of *kaizen*, or continual improvement, is based on just this approach—making small, incremental changes that lead to the fulfillment of one's goals. For example, many years ago, I'd donated a relatively large sum of money to a certain charity with the understanding that the money would be used to start a specific program dear to my heart. A year or so later, I discovered that the charity had spent the bulk of the money according to their own plans, almost completely disregarding my instructions. I went to lunch with a friend who had amassed a great fortune and recounted bitterly what had happened. "This is all your fault," she said. "You didn't communicate your vision well, you didn't set up milestones, you didn't monitor the charity's progress against them, and, given your expertise, you should have known better." I hadn't applied common sense in reevaluating my charitable decision.

The inevitable events that experts predict—pandemics, earthquakes, droughts, sea rise, and other disasters—take a long time to happen, but when they do, they happen fast. Scenario construction is good practice and preparation for handling the inevitable when it does take place. Such exercises will give you a good sense of what might occur, sooner or later, so you can make better decisions along the way.

Emerging Threats

There are many problems with the security products used today. Many antivirus solutions are only effective against known threats. On average, there are 350,000 new malware variants created every day. Relying on known malware solutions is an endless, no-win catch-up game. Also, many solutions take too long to detect and remediate attacks. The longevity of breaches has a direct impact on the extent of the damage. In case you're wondering, Ponemon Institute concluded that that the average time to identify and continue a breach in 2019 was 279 affected days. Even further, the more sophisticated solutions use AI algorithms that are too dependent on characteristics that are predetermined based on historical experience. Although machine learning is very accurate at detecting a wide range of known attack vectors, it doesn't work well when detecting never-seen-before attacks, particularly malware that has a unique solution. It seems that security products are always a step behind.

Further, emerging technologies often create new risks that haven't been encountered before and that also add complexity to existing risks. The interconnected nature of these risks creates a need to deal with the risks concurrently, rather than in isolation. For example, the increased reliance on interconnected systems by companies will amplify the impact of failure and threaten resilience. Taking this a step further with artificial intelligence, there are reputational, legal, and regulatory consequences as a result of algorithms that aren't totally aligned with social, ethical, cultural, or legal norms. For example, many organizations dropped their advertisements from a website after its programmatic advertising placed ads next to inappropriate content.

A bot is a software application that's programmed to do certain tasks. Bots are automated, which means they run according to their instructions without a human user needing to start them up. Bots often imitate or replace a human user's behavior. Typically, they do repetitive tasks, and they can do them much faster than human users could. Bad bots are programmed to break into user accounts, scan the web for contact information for sending spam, or perform other malicious activities. Bots have been used to amplify the damages from cyber incidents by acquiring large quantities of confidential data through excessive access and privileges.

Natural language generation tools and techniques will enable the processing, analyzing, and understanding of unstructured "big data" that companies will use to operate more effectively and pro-actively. However, the large scale spread of misinformation will also be enabled and will manifest in a variety of ways, including using social media to influence public opinion; creating false trends through paid online reviews; disseminating fake photos/videos that look real; and encouraging incorrect financial trading based on false perceptions.

Data processing on the internet in its current form is generally a centralized structure in which most of the data are collected and sent to large, remote data centers with good storage, processing, and net-work capabilities. This centralized model isn't sustainable, as the inter-net is shifting to massive numbers of wireless and remote devices that utilize large volumes of data that increasingly require faster response times. More computational, storage, and networking resources will need to be situated at the edge of networks (edge computing) to sig-nificantly reduce data traffic and improve response times for emerging applications such as smart homes, smart transportation, smart health, smart grids, and smart energy. However, edge computing will create new cybersecurity challenges for standard encryption, authentication, and access controls. For example, as a result, there will be a huge increase in denial-of-service attacks.

Use of Scenarios Based on Emerging Threats

Taking these potential threats into consideration, as well as actual real events, imagine this potential scenario involving artificial intel-ligence to understand what's possible and then what to focus on in terms of CyRMˢᴹ.

The real events, believe it or not, are several known cases in which criminals have taken over more than a million computers. The largest known botnet was Bredolab, which contained more than 30 million computers. It was created by a hacker network and made money by leasing out time on the hijacked computers to other criminal organizations. At its peak, it was able to send out more than three billion infected emails each day[1].

Now consider the following scenario[2]. First, an artificial intelligence system that has already taken over computers could gain access to the internet and hide thousands of backup copies, scattered among insecure computer systems around the world. It could then take over millions of unsecured systems on the internet, forming a large "botnet." This would be a vast scaling up of computational resources and provide a platform for escalating power. From there, it could gain financial resources (hacking the bank accounts on those computers). It would then be as powerful as a well-sourced criminal world, but much harder to eliminate. Please note that none of these steps involve anything mysterious—hackers and criminals have already done all of these things just using the internet. (My apologies for any misconceptions driven by Hollywood and the media that this requires robots.)

Applying CyRM℠

Based on this scenario's events, what would you monitor, and what potential managerial action steps would you take? For example, as a first step, it wouldn't be too difficult to monitor these attacks and get a sense of your own vulnerabilities against your more important assets that need to be protected. Second, perhaps hire web-filtering services that scan for websites exhibiting unusual behavior and block those websites from your users. Or perhaps standardize on a browser other than Google Chrome or Mozilla Firefox, which are two popular browsers (and, therefore, the browsers for which most malware is written). Again, it's important to think of decision-making process in terms of four steps: assessment of the situation, rules of the game, making the decision, and reevaluating after the fact. Remember, it's far better to make an error of commission—you looked at the issue, considered all your alternatives, then went the wrong way—as opposed to an error of omission, where you didn't even consider the potential problem.

CyRM ACTION POINTS: LOOKING TOWARD THE FUTURE

- Use scenario construction and analysis to predict the future and locate "trip wires."
- Make better decisions regarding risk via assessment of the situation and rules of the game, then make the decision and reevaluate after the fact.

Notes

1 Toby Ord, *The Precipice* (p. 365).
2 Toby Ord, *The Precipice* (pp. 146–147)

CONCLUSION

In far too many companies today, involvement with cybersecurity is an afterthought, bolted onto what people do each day to hopefully create a secure environment. We all know this approach doesn't work. Cybersecurity isn't approached as a business problem and then aligned with business needs. Also, no one is playing offense in cybersecurity—only defense, and companies are focused on yesterday's questions and threats that they don't control. We all know that real failures are often not used as learning experiences and aren't getting enough attention to effect change.

Even further, boards and C-level executives mistakenly think compliance will save them, but in reality, compliance doesn't equal appropriate levels of protection. Unfortunately, today a simple answer doesn't exist to the question, "Is my company's security adequate?" There's also a real disconnect between executive decision-making and IT professionals on cybersecurity, which is something that should keep more people up at night, because every new estimate has increased levels of new threats. Cybersecurity isn't just an important issue to get right—it's a "must have right" issue. There has to be a shift in the mindset from fighting yesterday's war to recognizing and getting ready to combat today's and tomorrow's threats.

It really takes an army, with all its varied roles and positions, to provide appropriate CyRM℠. There are plenty of roles for different people, the board, C-suite executives, the CISO, IT staff, risk management staff, auditors, and every employee of the company. It's an army of people from a variety of different backgrounds, wealth, and educational experiences, but everyone involved has a common purpose, which is why it functions so well.

We're all missing a common purpose in the cybersecurity realm: a real commitment to CyRM℠. To me, the importance of mastering the management of cybersecurity through CyRM℠ is like trying to explain the difference between involvement and commitment. It's like an egg and bacon breakfast—the chicken was involved, but the pig was committed. You must be committed. You must create a commitment to CyRM℠ in your company. Throughout this book I've emphasized that security should *not* be viewed as a technical problem handled by technical people. Too often, it's all about throwing money at technical solutions at the expense of executive engagement. Cybersecurity is a managerial issue. To be successful at this, you must approach security as a business problem and connect cybersecurity with business decision-making to impact business outcomes. Remember that CyRM℠, to effectively impact business outcomes, needs to consist of three prongs:

1. **Risk Management:** It applies the tenets of risk management to cybersecurity in order to take a broad view of risks across an organization to inform resource allocation, better manage risks, and enable accountability.

2. **CyberWellness℠:** It should encompass not only the firm as a whole, but every employee, who need to be responsible for the risks they undertake. This requires an active process with cybersecurity—just like physical wellness programs in which the company takes an active approach to promoting employees' good health.

3. **Cybersecurity as a Business Strategy:** Cybersecurity needs to be repositioned for what it really is: a growth enabler, and not just to reduce operational risks by eliminating the dangers posed by viruses and hackers. It also needs to enhance product integrity, customer experience, operations regulatory compliance, brand reputation, and investor confidence.

I wrote this book because I'm passionate about helping business leaders sleep better at night by equipping them with critical cyber risk management tools—CyRM℠ that protects their enterprises while enhancing strategic business growth. Four decades of experience as a financial leader for PwC, AllianceBernstein, Citibank, and others has provided me a grounding for balancing the realities of risk with the opportunities of business. Technology pervades all operations today, from how a business runs to how it delivers value and succeeds. Technology also threatens all these aspects. So, how do we flourish in this perilous environment?

My answer is to create a commitment to CyRM℠ in your company. I've laid out my approach to CyRM℠ and shown you—business leaders and IT managers alike—how to work together and succeed. In each chapter, I've highlighted what you need to know about navigating today's dangerous cybersecurity terrain, and outlined the proactive steps you need to take to prepare your company—and yourself —to survive, perhaps even thrive.

Management consulting pioneer W. Edwards Deming once said, "It is not necessary to change. Survival is not mandatory." We all know what he meant. Given the exponential velocity and intensity of change over the past few decades, it's even truer today than it was in Deming's day. Adapt or die.

APPENDIX A
GUIDING PRINCIPLES FOR CYBER RISK GOVERNANCE
Principles for Directors in Overseeing Cybersecurity

June 2018

The Directors and Chief Risk Officers Group  | the DCRO |
Directors and Chief Risk Officers Group

Leaders of the global risk governance community.

ABOUT THE DIRECTORS AND CHIEF RISK OFFICERS GROUP (THE DCRO)

The DCRO was formed in 2008 to focus on the top-level governance of risk in practice. Bringing together leading board members, chief risk officers, and other c-level officers whose jobs include a fiduciary responsibility for governance and risk management, the DCRO counts more than 2,000 members from large and mid-size for-profit and nonprofit organizations, coming from over 115 countries.

DCRO members participate in facilitated meetings, conference calls, benchmarking research, and governance councils that allow them to compare current practices with those adopted by fellow members, those being required by regulatory bodies, or those expected by investors.

Membership in the DCRO is strictly limited to active or recently active, board members, chief risk officers, or c-level executives with risk governance responsibilities.

For further information, or to provide comments on these guiding principles, please contact:

The Directors and Chief Risk Officers Group
e) info@dcro.org
w) www.dcro.org
t) +1-917-338-6631

Table of Content

Governance Council Co-Chairs   **92**

Introduction   **94**

Principles for Directors in Overseeing Cybersecurity

    I.   Cybersecurity as an Element of Enterprise Risk   94

    II.   Cybersecurity as a Strategic and Managerial Issue   97

    III. Broad Concepts of Cybersecurity   98

    IV. Understanding Exposure to Third-party Vendors   100

    V.   Developing a Corporate Culture that Values Cybersecurity   101

Conclusion   **104**

Guiding Principles for Cyber Risk Governance   **104**

DCRO Cyber Risk Governance Council Members   **105**

DCRO Cyber Risk Governance Council Co-Chairs

We offer special thanks to the co-chairs of the DCRO Cyber Risk Governance Council for their leadership on this initiative.

Roel C. Campos is a partner at the law firm of Hughes Hubbard & Reed in Washington, DC and is Chair of the Securities Enforcement practice. Mr. Campos' practice consists of advising senior management and boards in their most sensitive and complex issues. His practice often involves conducting internal investigations and defending matters involving financial regulators, such as the SEC, DOJ, CFTC, and FINRA. He also advises boards on items such as cybersecurity, governance, cryptocurrency and proposed rulemakings by financial regulators.

Beginning in 2002, Mr. Campos was appointed twice by President George W. Bush and confirmed by the U.S. Senate as a Commissioner of the SEC, serving until 2007.

Prior to being appointed to the SEC, Mr. Campos raised venture capital with partners, was a senior executive and operated a radio broadcasting company.

After attending Harvard Law School, he worked in Los Angeles for major law firms. Mr. Campos also served in the U.S. Attorney's Office in Los Angeles. He prosecuted major narcotics cartels and, in a celebrated trial, he convicted several kingpin cartel members for the kidnapping and murder of a DEA agent.

David X Martin is an expert in cybersecurity, having co-chaired a public/private initiative with the FBI and major corporations on intelligence sharing and best practices, consulted with the Central Bank of Israel on cybersecurity audits of Financial Institutions, chaired an information security committee for a public corporation, worked as a senior advisor on cybersecurity for Oliver Wyman, and published numerous articles on innovative approaches to managing cybersecurity. He is the co-managing director of cybXsecure, a cybersecurity consulting and development company.

Mr. Martin is an acknowledged expert on risk management and valuation issues and has extensive experience with investment strategies and operations, quantitative research, exchanges, and supervising trading desks. He was the founding Chairman of the Investment Company Institute's Risk Committee and Co-Chair of the Buy Side Risk Committee. He is a veteran financial executive whose 40-year career includes senior positions at PricewaterhouseCoopers (PWC), Citibank, and AllianceBernstein, where he served both as Chief Risk Officer and a Director of Sanford Bernstein LLC.

Mr. Martin is also an Adjunct Professor at NYU's and Fordham's Graduate Schools of Business, author of *Risk and the Smart Investor*, published by McGraw Hill in the fall of 2010, and author of *The Nature of Risk*, published by Amazon in 2012. He has also published numerous white papers on cybersecurity, compliance and risk, enterprise risk management, and corporate governance.

Mr. Martin serves as a member of the Sanctions Subcommittee of the US Department of State's Advisory Committee on International Economy Policy and as a Special Counselor to the Center for Financial Stability on cybersecurity and emerging risks.

Introduction

The purpose of this document is to provide boards of directors a set of Guiding Principles to enable the implementation of an effective cybersecurity program.

A director should understand the full range of cyber risks facing his or her company and encourage management to develop appropriate strategies tailored to the company's operating environment, risk profile, and long-term goals.

The specific needs of any effective cyber program include careful planning, smart delegation, and a system for monitoring compliance — all of which directors should oversee. It's no longer a question of *whether* a company will be attacked but more a question of *when* this will happen — and how the organization is going to prevent it. Smart network surveillance, early warning indicators, multiple layers of defense, and lessons from past events are all critical components of true cyber resilience. When things go wrong, whether in a major or minor way, the ability to quickly identify and respond to a problem will determine the company's ultimate recovery.

Cybersecurity cannot be guaranteed, but a timely and appropriate reaction can.

Longer term, the board should understand and consider the strategic business implications of cybersecurity, foster the right company culture surrounding security, and encourage the integration of cyber risk management practices into other governance and approval processes. In essence, the board should consider cybersecurity as a managerial issue, not just as a technical one.

I. DIRECTORS SHOULD VIEW CYBERSECURITY AS AN IMPORTANT ELEMENT OF ENTERPRISE RISK THAT THEY MUST OVERSEE.
    A. Identify the organization's essential assets ("crown jewels") that may be vulnerable to cyber attack.
    B. Identify which cyber risks to avoid, which to accept, and which to mitigate.
    C. Develop specific plans associated with each approach.

There are no offensive strategies in cybersecurity — only defensive ones. In addition, one cannot protect everything. It is therefore critical for board members to first determine which assets are most valuable, and second, to put in place the most effective strategy or strategies to protect these assets. Once the board ascertains the value of what needs to be protected, it can prioritize and allocate resources to avoid and mitigate cybersecurity threats. At that point, it can decide whether its cybersecurity budget is appropriate.

Defining an organization's risk capacity is a complex challenge because it requires all the personnel to be confident of the following items:

- Knowing their inventory of information assets is both complete and up-to-date;
- Being certain that the process used to prioritize the value of these assets is accurate and appropriate;
- Understanding the effectiveness of the key actions that have been taken to protect the most important assets, e.g., the crown jewels;
- Having a comprehensive command of the terms and conditions of other risk-mitigating items, such as insurance, with the corresponding knowledge of where insurance and other risk mitigation efforts will not be effective; and Possessing a deep understanding of the scale and robustness of the organization's business response and continuity plans that will be triggered in the event of a cyber incident.

The five elements listed above represent a sample of the component elements in the "risk capacity" calculation that board directors and senior management need to perform on an ongoing basis. The first three are critically important to directors to ensure they know what programs, investments and resources management has dedicated to protecting the most valuable holdings, because the theft, unauthorized access, or damage to these assets could represent an existential risk.

The last two also factor into the capacity calculation as inputs because the costs and benefits of mitigation actions, such as third-party cyber insurance and remote back-up facilities are also important.

These traditional risk management activities play an important role in how the organization assesses its capacity to endure or "weather" a pre-defined type of business continuity event.

The business continuity framework can help gain insight into the priority of the assets to be recovered after a cyber-breach has occurred. Of course, any "pre-defined" event estimate will likely not match what happens in reality, but an organization can use frequent simulated attacks in order to identify and assess whether other "less critical" assets are appropriately evaluated from a risk mitigation perspective.

To meet this duty of care, directors must be able to demonstrate that they have discharged their oversight function of cybersecurity in a reasonable common sense manner. To that end, directors should receive regular assessments and assurances from both the CEO and the CISO that the work being performed by the entire organization (i.e., not just the technology function) is highly focused on protecting the crown jewels and other high priority assets. These work initiatives should involve functional segmentation, robust identity access management, and higher levels of employee training, along with the leading-edge security practices at the network and end-point levels.

Also, acknowledging mistakes and learning from them leads to better decision making. Cybersecurity post mortems should be encouraged in briefings about the company's security model and vulnerabilities. There is no substitute for the proper deliberation and engagement of cybersecurity issues.

Of course, when developing new products and services, a company needs to strike the right balance between innovation and risk. In most cases, the more that security is increased, the less user-friendly and convenient the product becomes. Processes that should be reviewed for a cyber filter include strategic planning, M&A, product development, and capital allocation and budgeting. Even HR processes should have a cyber-filter to understand recruiting, leadership development, and cyber resource retention strategies.

II.   DIRECTORS SHOULD VIEW CYBERSECURITY AS A STRATEGIC AND MANAGERIAL ISSUE AND SHOULD THEREFORE HOLD MANAGEMENT ACCOUNTABLE FOR RECOMMENDING AND IMPLEMENTING THE OVERALL CYBER RISK MANAGEMENT STRATEGY AND POLICIES.

A.   Management should be accountable for reporting their actions and cyber breaches.

B.   Where appropriate, the board should require key executives to attest that certain important aspects of the cybersecurity plan have been executed.

C.   Promoting employee awareness and training is crucial.

D.   Third-party testing of cyber vulnerabilities can provide a high degree of deterrence.

E.   Boards should maintain an external team of professionals that are available for training and in crisis situation.

Directors must understand security through a broader lens than simply information technology (IT), since the potential harm to a company can be devastating.

Cybersecurity risk demands C-level accountability and board oversight to drive the agenda and manage empowered employees with the right skill sets.

Discussions about cyber risk management with the accountable corporate officer should be given regular and adequate time on board and board committee meeting agendas.

The accountable officer's leadership skills — communication and crisis management — should be considered equally, as they are often more important than technical skills. Clearly, in the day-to-day management of technology, or in a crisis, it is far better to have a skillful leader rather than a subject-matter expert.

The board should also create a self-assessment framework in terms (and language) that they fully understand to ensure that best industry practices are being implemented and real progress is being made. A strong focus on outcomes should replace pure activity- based reporting.

Directors need to promote a robust state of cybersecurity and resilience by encouraging appropriate interaction between all levels of management and subordinates.

It is well documented that approximately two-thirds of successful unauthorized cyber-attacks are directly attributable to the actions (or inactions) made by employees.

Therefore, improving awareness of employees to cyber risk exposures represents a meaningful opportunity to enhance an organization's overall cyber resilience.

Any measurable improvement to employee awareness through initiatives such as gamification and continuous training that is operational in nature would be highly accretive to an entity's capacity to protect and respond to a cyber-incident.

From a board director's perspective, it is important to receive in-depth analysis and evaluations of real and simulated incident response events that describe in detail the interactions between the various functional teams beyond the three described above. Such evaluations (perhaps performed by an independent third party) would provide insight into the organization's overall cyber resilience which is, at best, a continuously evolving objective.

An important part of cyber resilience entails establishing relationships with external experts and firms to support a more decisive response to a data breach. The post- breach environment is not the optimal time to be searching for required expertise or negotiating contractual terms, so having a team of external resources "at the ready" can speed recovery and resumption of operations. These external experts can include forensics, legal, communication, and systems remediation, among others. The approach to law enforcement (FBI and others) should also be considered in advance of an incident.

III. DIRECTORS SHOULD BE GUIDED BY TWO BROAD CONCEPTS OF CYBERSECURITY:
   A. Ensure that cybersecurity is managed within three lines of defense, and
   B. Ensure that cybersecurity is managed based on constantly reacting to gathering intelligence and promoting adaptation to the changing risk environment.

A. Three Lines of Defense

Cybersecurity requires an approach that goes beyond being the sole concern of the information security group. A preferred approach is a three-lines-of-defense model. The first line of defense, "risk identification and assessment," is the responsibility of the business units and information security teams. Therefore, they have the direct accountability for owning, understanding and managing cyber risks and making the directors aware of their risk assessments.

The second line of defense, "risk management," is the responsibility of the company risk management team to provide functional oversight from a strategic business perspective regarding the potential impact of threats, the determination of priorities, and the allocation of resources. The risk management team should also provide constructive, strategic business challenges to the first line's approach to cyber risk, ensuring that the right policies and procedures are in place, and that cybersecurity is effectively integrated into operational and enterprise risk. Again, periodic reports of the effectiveness of risk management should be provided to the board.

The third line of defense, "risk monitoring," is the responsibility of internal auditing to provide assurance to the board and senior management of the effectiveness of cyber risk governance for the enterprise.

These three lines of defense should be guided by an active, engaged board of directors that approves and oversees the firm's approach to cybersecurity, approving strategic decisions and priorities, while providing a credible and effective counterbalance to management.

B. Intelligence Driven Approach

The traditional approach to security relies on prevention strategies. It treats incident responses using an exception-based approach. In contrast, an intelligence-driven mindset is based on the assumption that the company has already been compromised and therefore the need exists to continuously evolve to stay ahead of the curve in terms of intelligence and incidents.

An adaptive security architecture allows decision making for security related issues that is based on the following: accurate threat modeling, a quantifiable asset valuation, and 'what if' scenarios that consider the deterrence factors of a security measure or process, as well as their cost. The right intelligence driven approach is based on prior experiences, current threat intelligence, understanding of breaches that have impacted other companies, trends, valuation of assets, and analysis of the safeguards to guard these assets constantly, including when controls fail.

Directors should also encourage the review of new technologies for access management, artificial intelligence, and distributive data that could potentially enhance the companies' cyber defenses.

IV. DIRECTORS SHOULD UNDERSTAND THE COMPANY'S EXPOSURE TO THIRD-PARTY VENDORS.

Third parties can be impactful to an operating environment, since boards and companies are not usually as attuned to cybersecurity risks from third parties as they are for their own businesses, even though third parties can create the same adverse, long-term effects.

Organizations that are laser-focused on delivering their missions through core competencies leverage the strengths of other providers and partners as a critical and viable business strategy. Companies manage hundreds, if not thousands, of vendor, third-party provider, and other types of outsourcing arrangements. These external parties are a primary source of incremental risk by creating new entry points into a company's technology environment. The sharing of data and communication is no longer fully in control of the internal operations of the organization, adding complexity and potential volatility to the operating environment.

Legal and other practical considerations can (and should) be employed to partition and mitigate the risk; however, the risk, no matter where it originates, will revert to the company in times of crisis or stress. Customers (corporate and individual) simply look to the company with which they are doing business for explanations and relief.

Many organizations are playing "catch-up" when it comes to vendor management. The ability to create a full inventory of vendor relationships is clearly "table stakes" in an overall program. The basics for a third-party program should include the following:

- Complete and comprehensive inventory of all third-party contracts
- Third-party exposures prioritized based on risk (including cyber) to the organization
- Clear assessment tools in place for the onboarding of any new relationships
- Ongoing, risk-adjusted monitoring processes in place to assess adherence to contract terms
- Third-party assessment of vendor practices through Service Organizational Control (SOC) reporting
- Joint disaster recovery testing with primary service providers

The activities should result in actionable and timely summarized board reporting; leveraging a technology-enabled vendor management solution is also a best practice.

An emerging trend is a fourth-party assessment to understand what activities have been further outsourced causing change to the risk profile for cybersecurity.

For cybersecurity risk, "risk-adjusted" is no longer purely a dollar filter, e.g., based on the financial size of the contract. With the proliferation of inexpensive applications and other narrow, but highly effective, tools to fully capture the risk profile of the relationship, other filters must also be used to understand the impact to the organization.

A strong third-party vendor management program does more than strengthen cybersecurity risk management — it can support spending decisions, contracting strategies, service levels, and other critical operational activities to support the attainment of core business objectives.

V. DIRECTORS SHOULD COMMIT TO DEVELOPING A CORPORATE CULTURE THAT PLACES A HIGH VALUE ON CYBERSECURITY.

A. With management, directors should define appropriate behavior for cybersecurity and then demonstrate clearly the importance the organization places upon strict adherence.

Risk culture is the glue that binds all aspects of risk-taking and risk management together through shared organizational values, beliefs, and attitudes. Through awareness and deliberate planning, risk culture can be proactively influenced to enhance an organization's risk and business management environments. Cybersecurity is no exception; establishing a strong cybersecurity culture is an essential component of any program, given that the vast majority of cyber risk can be initially traced to people and related behaviors, not technology.

However, most employees aren't interested in their personal digital security — much less their company's. Therefore, changing a company's culture to strengthen security is especially difficult — requiring a paradigm shift in order to keep pace with the evolving threats. Historically, anything to do with IT security was kept away from users by IT teams. Little wonder that users show no or little interest in the company's security.

But in reality, users should be the front line of data security. They create and handle the information — therefore they are best-placed to understand its value. Directors should request their management to develop interactive training and accountability programs that engage with users. Using modern game based training and thereafter monitoring how users and employees apply their training helps transform a company's culture into one where cybersecurity is everyone's concern.

Without a strong risk culture, even the best cybersecurity management framework would be vulnerable to weaknesses and failures. Given the continuously changing and quickly evolving cyber environment, embedding a strong cyber risk culture provides employees with principles and values to guide activities when policies are yet to be drafted or updated. Specific guidance may not always be available, relevant, or remembered. Indicators of a strong cybersecurity culture include:

- Clear and concise cybersecurity policy framework reflective of risks faced by the organization and the evolving operating environment;
- Board and leadership agendas prominently include cybersecurity;
- Cyber risk is not managed in a silo — discussions on cyber are woven into all management processes, such as new product approvals, merger due diligence, and third-party outsourcing arrangements;

- Continuous learning environment, including relevant and memorable training and tools to support strong cyber hygiene ranging from password protocols to anti-phishing campaigns to "bring your own device" policies;
- The existence of a safe environment for employees to bring forward risks or issues, employees need to know they are supported if they identify an unmitigated risk or emerging threat.

Another hallmark of a strong cybersecurity culture is that no one in the organization is exempt, including the board. Boards should demonstrate their knowledge of strong cybersecurity practices by participating in company cybersecurity training, avoiding personal e-mail for company business, and safeguarding (physically and electronically) confidential information.

B. Directors need to understand the legal and regulatory implications of cyber risks as they relate to their company's specific circumstances including their fiduciary duties and the overarching legal terrain.

High-profile incidents affecting Deloitte, Equifax, Facebook, and many others over the past year or so, remind us how quickly the risk of breaches and response to those events can impact a company's reputation. A breach of sensitive customer and company data and systems brings enormous scrutiny from shareholders and regulators and poses a significant risk to a firm's operations as well as to its stock price. Furthermore, under securities laws, directors are gatekeepers who have responsibilities to shareholders in preventing wrongdoing.

Of course, Directors have fiduciary duties of care, loyalty, and good faith to ensure to protect corporate assets, including customer information, as well as the firm's reputation and shareholder value. This includes ensuring the existence of an effective Cybersecurity Program that satisfies legal requirements and maintains multi-layered security measures that protect sensitive information from unauthorized modification, destruction, or disclosure — whether accidental or intentional. To meet their responsibilities, directors should schedule regular briefings from their General Counsel and/or outside lawyers to brief the directors on cybersecurity and privacy implications for federal, local, and state laws.

Conclusion

Public scrutiny after cyber-attacks and the regulators have made cyber-security a board issue and key responsibility. In crisis, the only thing people remember when it comes to judgement calls is the outcome. A good outcome is usually the result of a well- considered, disciplined process that demonstrates collective wisdom and commitment to corrective results.

Board meetings are an opportune time for corporate directors to reassess how they exercise their governance responsibilities with regard to the management of cybersecurity risk. In today's global cyber minefield, it is essential that boards of directors not just monitor performance, but incentivize excellence in this area.

Appendix
The DCRO Guiding Principles for Cyber Risk Governance

Principle 1: Directors should view cybersecurity as an important element of enterprise risk that they must oversee: identifying the company's essential assets that may be vulnerable to cyber attack, which cyber risks to avoid, accepts, or mitigate, and to develop specific plans associated with each approach.

Principle 2: Directors should view cybersecurity as a strategic and managerial issue and should therefore hold management accountable for recommending and implementing the overall cyber risk management strategy and polices.

Principle 3: Directors should be guided by two broad concepts of cybersecurity: ensuring that it is managed within "three lines of defense" and based on reacting and adapting to gathering intelligence and the changing risk environment.

Principle 4: Directors should understand the company's exposure to third-party vendors.

Principle 5: Directors should commit to developing the corporate culture that places a high value on cybersecurity.

DCRO Cyber Risk Governance Council Members

Co-Chairs

Roel Campos (US) | Partner, Chair of SEC Enforcement Defense Practice. Hughes Hubbard & Reed LLP; Former Partner, Head of Securities Regulation and Enforcement, Locke Lord LLP; Former Commissioner, U.S. Securities and Exchange Commission

David X Martin (US) | Expert Witness, Founder and Managing Partner, David X Martin, LLC; Special Counselor, Center for Financial Stability; Advisory Committee Member on International Economic Policy: Sanctions Subcommittee, U.S. Department of State; Adjunct Professor, NYU Stern School of Business; Former Chief Risk Officer, Alliance Bernstein; Former Chairman and CEO, Knightsbridge Capital Management; Former Enterprise Risk Manager, Citi

Council Members

Florence Angles (Switzerland) | Chief Risk Officer, REYL & Cie Ltd; founder of a Risk Manager Association in Switzerland: GIROS ; member of Club de lecture et de Présélection du Prix Turgot (Paris, France)

Masood Aziz (US) | Chief Risk Officer, FINCA International; Former Head of Compliance and Risk Management, State Street / PIMCO; Former Principal Advisor & Senior Diplomat – White House, State Department, Pentagon, and Congressional Leadership

Kevin Brock (US) | Founder, NewStreet Global Solutions, LLC; co-Founder, CyberXplore, LLC; Senior Fellow for Cybersecurity Strategy, The Center for Financial Stability; Former Assistant Director of the Directorate of Intelligence, Federal Bureau of Investigations (FBI); Former Principal Deputy Director, National Counterterrorism Center (NCTC)

Hannah Derry (US) | Global Head of Technology Risk Management, BlackRock; Former Director, Technology Services Division, Pacific Exchange (now NYSE Euronext)

William Ding (US/China) | President and CEO, SolarWind Capital & Risk Advisors, Former Chief Risk Officer, Woodbine Capital Advisors, LP; Former Chief Risk Officer, D. B. Zwirn & Co, LP;

Former Head of Risk Control, CDC IXIX Capital Markets North America; Former Co- Regional Director, PRMIA Boston and Former Steering Committee Member, PRMIA New York

Carol Gray (Canada) – Board Member and Member of Board People and Remuneration Committee, IFM Investors Pty (Melbourne); Board Member, ISPT/IFM International Property Management; Board Member and Chair, Board Risk Committee, Amex Bank of Canada; Former President, Equifax Canada; Past Board Member and Chair Ontario Realty Corporation; Past Board Member and Chair, Board Risk Committee, Infrastructure Ontario

Ignacio Fuentes (US) | Research Scholar, Digital Governance and Risk Management in Global Strategy and Block Chain in Digital Currency Initiative, Massachusetts Institute of Technology; Former Risk Governance Director, Santander Holdings USA

Jacinthe Galpin (US) | Director of Enterprise Resilience, Lowe's Companies; Former Chief Risk and Audit Officer, Department of Justice, Victoria, Australia; Former Head of Risk Management, Telstra Business

Marc Groz (US) | Co-Founder, CyberXplore; Former Managing Director, SPM LLC; Former Chief Investment Officer, Topos; Regional Director (CT), Professional Risk Managers International Association

Philip Harrington Jr. (US) | Independent Director, Willow Street Group; Independent Director, ProLink Solutions; Former EVP, Risk, and CAO, CA Technologies; Senior Managing Director, Brock Capital Group

Chris Jones (UK) | Chief Risk Officer, LME Clear Limited; Former Chief Risk Officer, LCH.Clearnet

Nicole Killen (Australia) | Chief Governance and Risk Officer, Mine Wealth + Welbeing; Non-Executive Director, Recreo Financial Technologies; Former Head of Governance and Trustee Services, Zurich Financial Services (Australia); served as Interim CEO of Mine Wealth + Wellbeing

David R. Koenig (US) | Founding Principal, The Governance Fund; Founder, The Directors and Chief Risk Officers Group; Former

Board Member and Chair, Professional Risk Managers' International Association; Former Board Member, Northfield Hospital & Clinics; Author, *Governance Reimagined: Organizational Design, Risk, and Value Creation*

Lloyd Komori (Canada) | Board Member, Chair Audit, Risk and Investment Committee ETFO – ELHT, Board member, Former Chair, Governance and Nominating Committee, Toronto Central Local Health Integration Network; Former Senior Vice President, Risk Management, OMERS Administration Corporation; Former Board Member, OMERS Administration Corporation; Former Chief Risk Officer, Ontario Power Generation; Founding Faculty Instructor, The Directors College

Lynn Mattice (US) | Distinguished Fellow, Ponemon Institute; Senior Fellow, George Washington University Center for Cyber and Homeland Security; Managing Director, Mattice and Associates; Chairman Emeritis, National Intellectual Property Law Institute; Board Member, International Security Management Association; Former Chief Security Officer, Boston Scientific

Cyril Maybury (Ireland) | Non-executive Director and Chair of Audit Committee, Generali PanEurope Ltd; Non- Executive Director and Chair of Audit and Risk Committee, Concern Worldwide; Pension Trustee of a number of pension funds; Former Chair, Business Law Committee, Consultative Committee of Accountancy Bodies – Ireland; Former partner in EY Ireland with various roles leading Audit, Risk Management, Fraud Investigation and Litigation Support and Expert Witness Services.

Julie Garland McLellan (Australia) | Board Advisor; Non-Executive Director, Suburban Land Authority; Non- Executive Director, Fitness Australia; Board Member, Professional Speakers Australia; Former Non-Executive Director and Chair, Audit Committee, Bounty Mining; Former Chair, Board of Directors, Oldfields Holdings Ltd.

Frank Morisano (US/China) | Chief Risk Officer, Industrial and Commercial Bank of China (ICBC) Limited, US Region and New York Branch; Non-Executive Director, ProfessioNext Limited (HK); Board Member, Ma Lee Advisory Limited (HK); Former Chief Risk

Officer, Capital G Bank; Former Chief Risk Officer, GMAC RFC; Former Board Member, Basis 100 Inc. (Canada)

Michael Nawrath (US) | VP – Information & Cloud Security, IptiQ Swiss Re; Former Senior Director of Global Information Security, World Fuel Services; Former Chief Information Security Officer, Direct Edge Stock Exchanges; Former Global Head of Information Security, Risk and Compliance for Networks, Credit Suisse

Braden Perry (US) | Co-Founder, Kennyhertz Perry LLC; Board of Directors, Kansas City Securities Association; Former Senior Vice President and Chief Compliance Officer, Mariner Holdings, LLC; Former Senior Trial Attorney, U.S. Commodity Futures Trading Commission

Vasilios Siokis (UAE) | Chief Risk Officer, Emirates Investment Authority; Former Chief Risk Officer, Cheyne Capital Management (UK) LLP; Former Head of Risk Management, Trafalgar Asset Managers

Stephen Soble (US) | Chairman and CEO, Assured Enterprises, Inc.; Former Chairman and CEO, API Development Group; JD Harvard Law; Developer of TripleHelix™ Cyber Risk Assessment system

Eric Staffin (US) | Chief Information Security Officer, Ipreo; Former Chief Risk Officer, S&P Global Market Intelligence, and Member of the S&P Global Risk Policy Committee

David Streliski (Canada) | Chief Risk Officer, Fiera Capital Corporation; Former Board Member, Professional Risk Managers' International Association (PRMIA); Co-Director, PRMIA Montreal

Mark Trembacki (US) | Managing Principal, Risk Management Levers, Inc.; Former SVP, Risk Integration and COO, Commercial Banking, BMO Financial Group; Adjunct Professor of Enterprise Risk Management, University of Illinois; Member, Chicago Steering Committee, PRMIA; Chair, Private Directors Association Cybersecurity Conference (2017)

Thank you to the sponsors of this document:

cybXsecure

Hughes
Hubbard
& Reed

The Directors and Chief Risk Officers Group
Leaders of the global risk governance community.

w) www.dcro.org
e) info@dcro.org
t) +1.917.338.6631

APPENDIX B

PRIMER ON CYBERSECURITY FOR BOARDS OF DIRECTORS

By Roel C. Campos and David X Martin

Hughes Hubbard & Reed LLP
A New York Limited Liability Partnership One Battery Park Plaza
New York, New York 10004-1482
+1 (212) 837-6000

How Do Directors Cope with their Obligations to Oversee Cybersecurity?

A Practical Primer For Boards of Directors in the Age of Equifax, Uber, et al.

By Roel Campos and David X Martin[1]

Many directors understand they have a responsibility to oversee cybersecurity at their companies. But more puzzling is what they should be doing now to contribute to the board's effort. What are the right questions they should be asking? Below we provide a short discussion of the major areas in cybersecurity compliance that you should be concerned with. We invite you to keep this article in your files for your director references and duties, and use the outline at the end of this article when discussing cybersecurity at board meetings.

Introduction

On September 7, 2017, one of the nation's largest credit monitoring agencies, Equifax Inc., announced that over 143 million customers' accounts had been breached in what may be the most significant cyberattack to impact U.S. consumers to date.[2] The number of affected individuals has since risen to an estimated 145 million people—all of whom likely had their personal information, including their names, Social Security numbers, birth dates, addresses, and driver's license numbers, compromised in the attack.[3]

Amidst the Equifax controversy, the U.S. Securities and Exchange Commission ("SEC") made some striking disclosures of its own. The newly-arrived SEC Chair, Jay Clayton, announced on September 20, 2017 that the SEC's own EDGAR filing system had been penetrated by cybercriminals months previously, leading to questions about the safety of such systems and the risk of insider trading by individuals with advance knowledge of sensitive, nonpublic company information.[4]

Other recent high-profile cyberattacks abound. Much to the chagrin of fans of the popular television show *Game of Thrones*, the HBO television network was breached in July 2017 by a group that pilfered over 1.5 terabytes of information, including show scripts and full episodes of several prominent shows.[5] And on September 25, 2017, *The Guardian* revealed that Deloitte LLP, one of the "Big 4" accounting firms (whose advisory clients include large companies and government departments) had been the victim of a breach and had its internal email system compromised.[6] Deloitte has since notified six of its clients whose information may have been "impacted" by the breach, and an internal investigation into the incident is ongoing.[7]

In one of the more salacious stories, recent revelations from Uber Technologies, Inc. detail a 2016 breach of the ride-sharing company's systems, during which hackers stole the names, email addresses, phone numbers, and drivers' license numbers of millions of Uber's customers and drivers. Not only did Uber fail to disclose the breach for over a year—but it also purportedly paid a "ransom" to the hackers in exchange for a promise by the hackers to delete the purloined data and keep the cyber incident quiet.[8]

Although cybersecurity is not a new challenge for boards of directors, the sheer scope and volume of recent events suggest that we may be experiencing a watershed moment when it comes to directors' responsibility to oversee, and managers' duty to implement, adequate cybersecurity systems at companies. Following Equifax's public disclosure of the cyberattack affecting its systems, observers learned a good deal about what potentially went wrong at the company—including a series of red flags that senior managers and boards of directors at other companies may learn from. Taken together, the recent breaches reveal

---

Cyber Breaches by the Numbers. The 2017 Data Breach Investigations Report by Verizon provides useful data on the type and frequency of common cyber breaches. For example, the report found that cyber breaches often involve:

- Some form of hacking (62%)
  - o stolen or weak credentials (81% of hacking-related breaches)
- Malware (51%)
  - o malicious email attachments (66% of all malware installed);
- Physical actions (8%)
- "Social" tactics (43%)
- Privilege misuse (14%)

Source: Verizon, 2017 Data Breach Investigations Report 3, (10th ed. 2017), http://www.verizonenterprise.com/verizon-insights- lab/dbir/2017/.

---

a series of lessons and warnings that boards of directors simply cannot afford to overlook anymore.

The first lesson is that companies must pay attention to routine alerts warning of cyber vulnerabilities in the company's systems and in software the company uses. In Equifax's case, hackers apparently exploited a known network vulnerability in the Apache Struts web-application software, which Equifax used to build its web applications. The U.S. Department of Homeland Security's United States Computer Emergency Readiness Team ("US-CERT") notified Equifax and many others of this vulnerability and the need to patch the software on March 8, 2017. Although the company disseminated the US-CERT notification internally by email and requested that appropriate personnel apply the patch, the patch was apparently not installed, or not installed correctly, and follow-on scans of the system one week later failed to reveal the error.

The second lesson is that companies must ensure they have appropriate systems in place to escalate information about potential cyber incidents and ensure, for example, that the general counsel imposes a freeze on trading in the company's securities by individuals with insider knowledge of material breaches during key windows. In Equifax's case, it was revealed that several executives had traded in the company's stock after the breach had been reported internally but before the public had knowledge of the breach. This raised questions about possible insider trading and a lack of internal controls at a time when Equifax was already subject to intense public scrutiny over the breach itself. (The executives have since been cleared of wrongdoing by a special committee at Equifax tasked with analyzing the breach.)[9]

The third lesson is that boards of directors must have a public response plan in place should a catastrophic cyberattack occur on their watch. Equifax's public handling of the incident has been widely criticized from virtually all angles. Many, for example, have complained that it took the company a full month to disclose the incident publicly after the company first learned of the breach in late July 2017. Others have ridiculed Equifax for directing consumers, in the immediate aftermath of the breach, to an insecure "spoofed" website mimicking the one Equifax had set up to engage with customers anxious to learn if their personal information had been compromised. Still others lamented that the company appeared to be in "PR mode" following the breach, and made missteps such as offering credit moni-toring services to affected individuals for a fee, rather than free of charge. (The company later moved to offer victims free access to credit monitoring services, but forced those customers to agree to lengthy arbitration provisions which would limit the customers' ability to sue Equifax in connection with the services. Equifax later abandoned the arbitration clause after a public outcry.)[10] All of these events suggest that Equifax was ill- prepared to deal with the public fallout that would predictably ensue following a disclosure of this magnitude.

The fourth lesson is that companies should carefully consider when and how they will disclose a breach. The recent disclosures of cyber incidents at Equifax and Uber provide valuable guidance to boards of directors in this regard. A company must consider not only its legal disclosure obligations, but also the court of public opin-ion when assessing when, and what, to disclose. In a similar vein, some have pointed out that the SEC's public disclosure of a cyber incident involving its EDGAR database came months after internal reports of the event were raised, illuminating just how difficult it is for any actor— including those charged with overseeing disclosure-based conduct—to balance the competing needs for a speedy public disclosure and a thorough internal review. The SEC's own less-than-ideal response to a cyber breach (and a resulting delayed cyber disclo-sure) raises questions about how the agency will pursue companies for cyber-related disclosures in the future and balance the compet-ing needs for prompt disclosures on one hand, and rigorous internal reviews on the other.

A final lesson is that companies should be aware of the risks posed when third parties handle sensitive company data. The events at Deloitte provide yet another data point and reinforce the notion that companies must be concerned not only with their own cyberse-curity systems, but also those of third-party vendors and consultants (and even, perhaps, the government) when those entities handle sensi-tive company data.

Given these recent high-profile events, we discuss below a series of practical considerations and principles that a board member can use to help the board build an effective and dynamic cybersecurity program at his or her company. These considerations will also help a director test the current status and effectiveness of the cybersecurity program.

Practical Considerations for Directors

As a first principle, directors should understand their fiduciary duties when it comes to cybersecurity and the overarching legal terrain guiding their companies. In addition to business and reputational risks, a lapse in cybersecurity can result in significant legal consequences for a company, its management, and, in certain cases, its board of directors. Companies must be aware of and understand various federal and state statutes, some of which regulate specific industries or types of sensitive information.

Companies must also be aware that federal and state regulators, such as the SEC, DOJ, and FTC, may increasingly focus on cybersecurity when enforcing otherwise non-cyber-specific laws, such as federal consumer protection and securities laws. In addition, directors must also heed the risk of shareholder and consumer lawsuits,

---

Understanding Motive. What motivates perpetrators of cyber breaches? The answer is straightforward in some cases, and more complicated in others. (In short, "it depends.") Below is a basic framework a director may consider.

Financial

- Attacker wishes to obtain sensitive non-public market-changing information to facilitate profitable trades using that information.
- Attacker wishes to obtain personally identifiable information to facilitate identify theft.
- Attacker wishes to obtain corporate or trade secrets to undercut competitors or other market participants.

Espionage / Surveillance

- State actor wishes to obtain personal or proprietary information for political or economic uses.
- The unusual case: State actor wishes to retaliate against a company or shut down controversial operations (e.g., the 2014 hack of Sony Pictures).

Ideological

- "Hacktivist" or similar group seeks to obtain nonpublic information in order to release it to the public on ideological grounds.

---

which are commonly initiated in the wake of the disclosure of cybersecurity incidents. As discussed below, the company's general counsel and internal cyber personnel should schedule regular briefings for the board to assess these developments.

1. Take Stock of Existing Cybersecurity Risks and Prioritize

Cybersecurity is a "first order" risk in many industries. If they have not already done so, boards of directors should invest in a formal briefing to discuss the range of existing cybersecurity risks facing their companies and weigh the pros and cons of various mechanisms that may help protect the company's most valuable assets in light of those risks. The board should first identify the company's most valuable assets and evaluate how those assets might be compromised by a cyber incident. For some companies, their most valuable asset is customers' private financial information, personally identifiable information, or possibly health records. For others, it might be intellectual property, or perhaps a proprietary database, or even a cache of sensitive emails. Any cybersecurity program must be geared towards protecting these most important corporate assets.

Directors should have a baseline understanding of the various types of cyber breaches that may occur on company systems and be familiar with the technical terms frequently used in the industry. Common cyber incidents at companies may range from malware to phishing attacks, and from unpatched software vulnerabilities to advanced persistent threats ("APT"). Additionally, vulnerabilities in a company's physical security may allow actors to penetrate the company's cyber defenses.

According to a recent survey by Diligent Corporation presented at the NYSE Governance Services Cyber Risk Forum, **60% of directors say they regularly use personal email to conduct company business,** *while* **49% report it is a "common practice" to download board books and company documents on personal devices**.
Source: NYSE Governance Services & Diligent, The Price of Convenience: Communications, Cyber Risk, and Cybersecurity Practices of Corporate Boards (2017) , https://www.nyse.com/publicdocs/Diligent_Board_Comm_Report_2017.pdf.

While it is not necessarily incumbent on the board to study the technical mechanisms of a cyberattack or response thereto, the board should have enough familiarity with these concepts to enable productive discussions with management and effective oversight of the company's cybersecurity program.

In taking stock of existing cybersecurity risks, boards should pay close attention to trends and recent events in their particular industry and impacting companies of a similar size. Particular types of cyber-attacks appear more frequently in some industries, and less in others. If you are a small retailer, for example, your most pressing cybersecurity concern may be point of sale intrusions, where attackers exploit weaknesses in remote- access applications (often provided by third-party vendors) in order to siphon your customers' credit card payment information.[11] On the other hand, if you are a large financial institution with sprawling and accessible physical infrastructure (*i.e.*, ATM machines), then you may face a broader range of cyber vulnerabilities, including the risk of "skimming" attacks on individual nodes in the network.[12]

Directors should also have a broad understanding of who or which groups are most likely to target their companies, and for what purpose. As a starting point, the *2017 Data Breach Investigations Report* by Verizon ("2017 Verizon Report") suggests that the majority of cyber breaches are perpetrated by external threat actors (75%), while a smaller percentage are perpetrated by insiders, such as employees or former employees (25%).[13] A growing number of breaches can be traced to state-affiliated actors (18%), while a smaller percentage involves business partners (2%).[14]

Once the board has a good handle on the company's existing cyber threat profile, it should prioritize strategies to mitigate the risk of an actual cyber breach. An effective director will help the company determine which assets are most valuable and evaluate the key controls in place to protect them.

He or she will also plan for contingencies and ensure there is an appropriate response framework in place to deal with potential cyber incidents. Part of this exercise will inevitably entail reviewing the company's budget related to cybersecurity to determine whether it is appropriate in light of existing threats and the robustness of existing company systems. (Keep in mind that it is less expensive to prevent a problem than it is to fix it.)

One key takeaway is that there are no offensive strategies in cyber-security—only defensive strategies. In addition, you cannot protect everything. Even the most technologically advanced organization in cyber—the National Security Agency ("NSA")—could not protect its deepest secrets.[15] It is therefore critical for the company to (1) reflect on which company assets are most valuable, (2) determine which systems are most vulnerable, and (3) consider what available mechanisms and strategies are both business-critical and cost-effective in view of this calculus.

2.   Assess Corporate Culture and Set the Right Example

Firms that really "get it" in cybersecurity have adaptive cultures. However, most corporate cultures do not change quickly—they evolve at a slow pace. As a result, the security culture in many organizations has not kept pace with the threat landscape in which they operate.

Security needs to be framed as a critical enabler that helps the company deliver its promise to customers. It also needs to be viewed by all levels of the company's workforce as a shared endeavor based on *teamwork, not surveillance.*

Also consider the "tone at the top" of your company and the messages that are being sent to employees related to cybersecurity practices. Encourage senior management to cultivate an environment where everyone has shared responsibility for cybersecurity. Ideally, employees should have a direct line of communication with someone in the company's chief information security officer's ("CISO's") department and understand they can reach out to that person for judgment and hassle-free guidance.

It is also crucial that company management invest in quality employee training related to cybersecurity. It is now considered a best practice that employees receive a general security awareness training, which may focus largely or exclusively on cybersecurity.

Also, training should not be a "one-and-done" exercise. The CISO's department or the GC should regularly provide updates to employees via email on recent developments in cybersecurity and issues they should be aware of. This is the kind of constant reinforcement that cultivates a true culture of cyber "wellness."

A good place to start in evaluating a company's cybersecurity culture is to review the company's written and formal guidance on the use and protection of company systems. Does the company, for example, have a written policy regarding employees' use of personal email to conduct company business? How is that policy implemented and observed? Does the board abide by the same standard, or are there exceptions made? Ideally, directors will be able to lead by example. Understand that as a director, you may be a particularly attractive target for a cyber breach, as it is known that directors often use personal devices to download board books and communicate about sensitive, non-public company information.

In all, a culture of cyber wellness needs to become a strategic focus embedded in the day-to-day operations and core values of the company. The new paradigm should be that cybersecurity is an ongoing risk that needs to be managed by everyone in the organization. When employees (of your company or of other companies) make missteps on this front, use these experiences as textbook examples of what not to repeat—anywhere in the firm. Because breaches often result in legal action, the board should include lawyers in their discussions and make sure their efforts to change corporate culture are seasoned with a legal perspective.

Does Board Membership Itself Require Cyber Expertise? On March 7, 2017, a bill was introduced in the U.S. Senate that would require the SEC to issue a rule requiring registered issuers to disclose whether any member of its board of directors "has expertise or experience in cybersecurity," and if no director has such expertise, "to describe what other cybersecurity steps taken by the [company]" were considered by those in charge of identifying and evaluating nominees for the board of directors, such as a company's nominating committee. The bill, titled *The Cybersecurity Disclosure Act of 2017* (S. 536), was introduced by Sen. Mark Warner (D-Va.), Sen. Jack Reed (D-R.I.) and Sen. Susan Collins (R-Me.).

> If passed into law, it would allow the SEC, in coordination with the U.S. Department of Commerce's National Institute of Standards and Technology, to define terms such as "expertise."
>
> **Source: S. 536, 115th Cong. § 2 (2017).**

After assuring that the tone at the top is one of integrity and effective compliance, the board should turn to strategic considerations.

3. Engage Key Cybersecurity Personnel

The board should participate in selecting key personnel, such as the CISO. They should also ensure that adequate systems are in place to monitor those individuals' performances. In times past, companies often delegated responsibility for cybersecurity to the company's chief operations officer or chief technology officer. Consider the officer who currently has primary responsibility for cybersecurity at your company. Is that person C- suite level? Is cybersecurity only one of many, pressing demands they are currently juggling? If the answer to the first question is "no," and the second "yes," you may consider creating a new role in the form of a CISO.

The board should also consider the internal reporting structure for the CISO (or other officer with primary responsibility for cybersecurity) to ensure this individual has the independence and authority needed to succeed in this mission-critical role. The CISO may report to the company's chief information officer, chief operations officer, chief technology officer, or even the chief executive officer—but in any case the CISO should have access to senior management and the board as needed. Company management should also consider establishing an information security committee chaired by the company's CISO, and invite C-suite officers to attend the committee's meetings. Directors, for their part, should understand who fills the CISO role and engage directly with that individual as appropriate.

4. Evaluate Risk Management Strategies

From the board's perspective, the key to effective oversight is to hold senior management responsible for articulating and monitoring the

---

Consider engaging an **independent third party to conduct an attack and penetration assessment** *at your company. This is an effective way to test your company's current systems and monitor existing vulnerabilities— without experiencing an actual incident.*

---

company's strategy and risk tolerance related to cybersecurity. In most cases, board members should have their noses, but not their fingers, in the company's cybersecurity program.

One area where boards can, and should, play a crucial role is in developing the company's strategic plan related to cybersecurity. Following this initial effort, the board should oversee company management in implementing the strategic plan.

The board should also work with management to develop a cyber incident "response playbook" mapping out how the company would respond to various contingencies in the event of a breach or serious cyber incident impacting company systems. For example, in the wake of the Uber scandal, a company may want to consider how it would approach a ransom request, weighing the pros of potentially mitigating some of the damage associated with a breach against the cons of rewarding criminal behavior in this manner. Any such analysis should be flexible enough to take into account of-the-moment law enforcement recommendations and a legal analysis of the company's disclosure obligations. To avoid an Equifax problem, the public response plan should designate an internal and external team of professionals to investigate the causes and make appropriate disclosures.

There are various frameworks that company management can use to develop appropriate risk management strategies related to cybersecurity. For example, in October 2013, the U.S. Department of Commerce, National Institute of Standards and Technology ("NIST") issued for comment a set of voluntary standards and best practices for reducing cybersecurity risk. The final version was released in February 2014, titled *Framework for Improving Critical Infrastructure Cybersecurity*.[16]

The NIST framework includes five "functional areas," which directors may consider in developing an overarching cybersecurity plan for their companies. These functions include:

1 **Identify**: Develop the organizational understanding to manage cybersecurity risk to systems, assets, data, and capabilities.
2 **Protect**: Develop and implement the appropriate safeguards to ensure delivery of critical infrastructure services.
3 **Detect**: Develop and implement the appropriate activities to identify the occurrence of a cybersecurity event.

4 **Respond**: Develop and implement the appropriate activities to take action regarding a detected cybersecurity event.
5 **Recover**: Develop and implement the appropriate activities to maintain plans for resilience and to restore any capabilities or services that were impaired due to a cybersecurity event.[17]

Guidelines from the SEC also provide valuable assistance to directors, given the agency's considerable influence in markets. Cybersecurity has long been a priority of the SEC's National Exam Program, which is overseen by the Office of Compliance Inspections and Examinations ("OCIE"). In August 2017, OCIE posted a risk alert highlighting the results of its Cybersecurity 2 Initiative.[18] Although this initiative focuses only on broker dealers, investment advisers, and funds—entities over which the SEC has primary jurisdiction—the findings of OCIE provide a template that directors of companies in other industries and their management can use to evaluate their own efforts in cybersecurity.

As part of the Cybersecurity 2 Initiative, OCIE assessed how companies managed their cybersecurity programs in the following areas:

i) governance and risk assessment;
ii) access rights and controls;
iii) data loss prevention;
iv) vendor management;
v) training; and
vi) incident response.[19]

From a broad perspective, OCIE found that while firms were doing more to establish cybersecurity programs, they were not doing enough to maintain and update those programs in light of the constantly changing cyber threats and attacks.[20] For example, OCIE noted that

---

Determining when and what to disclose can be even trickier when law enforcement is involved.

Oftentimes when a cyberattack occurs, law enforcement will need time to investigate before the breach is made public.

Experienced legal professionals should be consulted.

---

nearly all firms had plans that address access incidents, such as denial of service incidents and unauthorized intrusions; however, less than two–thirds of advisers and funds surveyed appeared to adequately maintain such plans.[21]

5.   Develop Systems to Monitor Cybersecurity Efforts

Directors should approach monitoring their companies' cybersecurity efforts like ongoing maintenance of machinery. Regular checks and adjustments will be needed, and it is not a one-time exercise. Technical means for conducting and preventing cyberattacks will constantly evolve.

Moreover, old tactics and systems may be deemed irrelevant or insufficient as the company moves towards different operating systems or expands its business portfolio.

Accordingly, it is wise for directors to have a standing review of the company's cybersecurity program at quarterly meetings, at the very least. There should also be a procedure in place for briefing the board more frequently if new and serious issues emerge.

The company's board minutes should accurately reflect when cybersecurity is discussed at such meetings so that the board's diligence is documented and demonstrated. Boards should also regularly receive a cybersecurity scorecard that highlights the company's progress mitigating cyber risk, including external metrics, gap remediation, emerging risks, trade-offs, and other issues. The scorecard does not need to include highly technical key performance indicators to be effective. Instead, examples of good metrics for the board include: customer satisfaction (customer system downtime caused by information security incidents); reputation (number of information security incidents reported in the media); and financial (information security budget as a percent of IT budget).

Key takeaway from Equifax: Ensure there are appropriate systems in place at your company to escalate reports of cybersecurity incidents to company management, and ultimately to the board, as appropriate.

As an important principle, boards should ensure that management and company employees collect, analyze, and share data regarding cybersecurity incidents—both large and small—to help inform the effectiveness of ongoing cybersecurity efforts. The company should also prioritize collecting, analyzing, and sharing internally any information the company may receive from government, private, or nonprofit sources regarding cyber vulnerabilities and possible exposure.

Following Equifax, it is important for all companies to take a hard look at their information escalation protocols. Who is informed when a possible cyber incident is first picked up on the company's radar?

Oftentimes, more junior employees will be best- placed to observe the first signs of a cyber breach. When it comes to installing critical software patches— such as in Equifax's case—ensure there are systems in place for appropriate supervision and peer review such that one person's human error does not result in a catastrophic (and preventable) breach.

Directors should also ensure the company has a system in place to encourage employees and management to learn from past mistakes.

Acknowledging mistakes and learning from them leads to better decision making. Cybersecurity post mortems should be encouraged in briefings about the company's security model and vulnerabilities. When a mistake occurs, this is also a good time to consult a lawyer. Certain mistakes come with legal responsibilities. For example, a company may have to disclose cybersecurity risks and adverse cyber events to its shareholders. Boards should make sure any post mortem, and any policy that grows out of it, include the necessary legal response.

6. Review Adequacy of Cyber Disclosures

More and more public companies are describing cybersecurity as a risk in their financial disclosures each year.[22] But what to disclose, and when to disclose it, remain thorny issues for many.

Equifax received significant criticism for waiting until September to disclose a breach it discovered in late July. But companies and regulators alike are realizing that there is a major tension between disclosing early on one hand, and waiting to learn all material facts in order to avoid making misleading or inaccurate disclosures, on the other. The SEC itself was subject to criticism for its perceived missteps in handling the EDGAR data breach. The SEC first reported that no personally identifying information was taken; it later had to revise these statements.[23] Also, the breach happened in 2016, but was reported to the public in September 2017.

It is critically important for companies to have appropriate escalation protocols in place. Do not lose precious time waiting for the report of a breach to slowly make its way up the chain to decision-makers. Instead, any time between a material breach and disclosure should be well spent investigating the facts and analyzing the issues.

The SEC has provided some guidance in this area. In 2011, the SEC's Division of Corporation Finance published guidance for public companies concerning disclosure obligations related to cybersecurity threats and adverse cyber events.[24] The guidance recommends that material information regarding cyber risk and adverse cyber events should be disclosed if necessary to make other disclosures not misleading. In particular, a company should review its cyber risks in light of the severity and frequency of prior cyber events. Companies should also consider the adequacy of their cyber defenses in light of the risks present in its particular industry. Companies should avoid generic risk factor disclosure and instead should consider their unique facts and circumstances. For example, a disclosure that a threat *may* occur may be insufficient if a company has *already* experienced that threat. A company should also consider including a discussion of cyber risks and incidents in the management discussion and analysis (MD&A) portion of its regular filings if the costs or consequences associated with the cyber risk or incident are likely to have a material effect on the company's financial condition.

While the SEC has yet to dip its toe, other regulators have already been active in enforcing cyber-related disclosure obligations. For example, in August 2017, Uber settled charges brought by the Federal Trade Commission ("FTC") relating to a 2014 breach. The FTC alleged that the company made deceptive claims about its efforts to safeguard customer information and failed to undertake "reasonable, low-cost measures" to prevent unauthorized access to customers' personal data. Meanwhile, the FTC has confirmed that it is currently scrutinizing Uber's response to the 2016 breach, which the company only recently disclosed.[25]

The FTC also previously brought a case against Oracle for disclosure issues, claiming that the company failed to inform consumers that newer software updates would not automatically remove older (and potentially exploitable) versions of Oracle's Java software. Last year the Consumer Financial Protection Bureau ("CFPB") ordered Dwolla, Inc., a company that operates an online payment system, to pay a penalty and improve its security practices after the company allegedly misrepresented to consumers that its networks were "safe" and "secure," and that its data security practices "exceed" or "surpass" industry security standards.

Additionally, while there is no national "data breach notification" law as of yet, the vast majority of states have enacted laws that require entities to notify affected individuals in the event of certain cybersecurity breaches involving sensitive consumer and personally identifiable information.[26]

Uber may well be the most egregious example of delayed disclosure and "what not to do." The company failed to notify regulators and individuals affected by the breach for nearly a year, possibly in violation of state notification laws. Moreover, Uber allegedly made non-disclosure of the breach a condition of its ransom payment to the cybercriminals, only further perpetuating the image of a cover up.

Several states' attorneys general have already initiated investigations into the breach.

The key takeaway is that it is absolutely essential for companies to review the adequacy and timeliness of their cyber disclosures on an ongoing basis. There is no "one-size-fits-all" answer. The advice of experienced disclosure counsel is crucial.

7.   Understand Third-Party Vulnerabilities

If recent events have taught us anything, it is that a company's cybersecurity protocols are all for naught if the company fails to ensure that third-party service providers also implement adequate cyber risk management systems. All too often, the entry-point for the cyber criminals is a third party who has access to the company's systems or nonpublic data.

Home Depot, for example, is still feeling the reverberations from a 2014 cyber incident in which hackers took advantage of a security flaw in a third- party payment processor to steal email and payment information of more than 50 million Home Depot customers. Hackers similarly used a third-party vendor to access Target's customer database in 2013 and stole payment information from approximately 40 million customers.[27]

The recent example of Deloitte demonstrates why companies should pay attention to professional service firms in particular when it comes to third-party cyber risk. Professional service firms—such as law firms, auditors, and consultants—are particularly vulnerable because their databases and cloud computing applications often contain sensitive information from many different clients and business partners, all in one convenient location for cyber criminals to exploit. The information professional service firms possess is an appealing target for cyber criminals because it is relatively easy to monetize through illegal trading. Such information may also be an attractive target for hacktivists.

The 2015 "Panama Papers" scandal was one of the first major incidents to shed light on law firm cyber vulnerabilities. The compromised firm, Mossack Fonseca, had helped hundreds of U.S. clients establish offshore businesses. The hack compromised the sensitive information of Mossack Fonseca's high-profile clients, dating as far back as the 1970s, and left many companies who had worked with the firm exposed.[28] We see a similar set of circumstances currently unfolding in the "Paradise Papers" scandal involving the release of the law firm Appleby's confidential client information.[29]

Because third parties often have access to highly sensitive company information, they should be subject to a rigorous third-party cyber risk assessment before companies engage them.

Directors do not need to be aware of the nitty gritty details of each and every contract for services, but they should ensure that the company has a written vendor risk management policy in place for addressing third parties' access to company systems and sensitive non-public data. At bottom, the policy should ensure that management conducts proper due diligence and is aware of the risks of doing business with particular vendors. The company should also routinely reassess third-party risk and ensure that third-party service providers are in fact complying with their obligations.

Boards should also be aware of the risks associated with providing the government with sensitive nonpublic information. The breach of the SEC's EDGAR database raises serious questions about how much sensitive company data should be held by market regulators and whether the government, with its limited resources, can protect such data.[30] When possible, companies should consider providing information on encrypted physical media versus through secure file transfer.

8. Consider Methods to Transfer Cyber Risk

Cybersecurity is not a problem to be solved—it's an ongoing risk to be managed and, where prudent, transferred. As part of the risk management effort, the board should carefully review existing contracts with third-party vendors and insurance policies.

These agreements must clearly state who is liable and what is covered in case of a breach.

Although cyber insurance is still in its nascent stages, with little actuarial data, it is one of the fastest growing types of coverage among U.S. companies— and with good reason.[31] The costs associated with a cyberattack can be game-changing for a company. A recent study conducted by Ponemon Institute shows that the average cost globally of a data breach is $3.62 million.[32] Victims of large-scale cyberattacks could expect to add several zeroes to that figure, as damage to reputation, costs of notification, and protracted litigation quickly add up.

In its annual report filed with the SEC earlier this year, Target Corporation reported that it had incurred $292 million in cumulative expenses in connection with the 2013 data breach of its systems, which resulted in the massive theft of customers' credit card information.

According to the company, this total amount was offset, in part, by $90 million in insurance payments.[33] Similarly, early this year, FedEx's Dutch subsidiary was hit by the "NotPetya" virus, which caused a temporary shut-down in the company's operations and led to a $300 million hit to its quarterly profit.[34] FedEx did not have insurance coverage for the attack, and FedEx's chief financial officer has since revealed that the incident triggered an internal re- evaluation as to whether the company should purchase cyber insurance moving forward.[35]

In addition to the obvious potential benefit of a monetary insurance recovery, seeking cyber insurance may result in ancillary advantages for companies. A company that is in the market for cyber insurance will be incentivized to use best practices, as premiums will be based, at least to some extent, on the company's effective use of protective measures. The application process alone may require an in-depth evaluation of a company's existing cyber program. Through this process, the company may gain a better appreciation of its own cyber risks and opportunities. Boards should also be aware that insurance carriers often offer tools to help companies respond to cybersecurity incidents and mitigate post-breach losses, should the need arise.

Boards are commonly in a position to have the final say on whether a company should purchase cyber insurance. Making this decision as a board may require navigating some new terrain. You must determine what is, and should, be covered, and what is not, and need not, be covered. You also need to determine whether a particular premium is fair. One question boards should ask is whether existing insurance policies may cover certain events.

Traditionally, most commercial general liability (CGL) policies did not contain cyber "exclusions"; however, these days, insurers may be more likely to include such provisions in their policies. Directors should ensure there are no critical gaps in coverage and consider what coverage makes the most sense based on their company's own risk profile (for example, coverage options may include coverage for costs of data breaches; extortion; forensic analyses; theft; litigation costs and expenses; and business interruption, to name a few). Boards should also confirm that their directors and officers (D&O) policies include coverage of cybersecurity-related events.

9.   Stay on Top of Developments

There is nothing stagnant about cybersecurity. The hacks are ever evolving, and defensive practices that are industry standard one month may be obsolete the next. Legislators and regulators, in turn, strive to keep pace with new laws and regulations, spurred in no small part by public outcry following high-profile breaches. The State of New York, for example, has responded to the recent Equifax breach by proposing regulation to expand the state's first-of-its-kind cybersecurity rules, which currently require all financial institutions in New York to register with the state and implement programs to protect consumer data, among other things.[36] The new regulation would extend the requirements to credit reporting agencies.[37] New York's Attorney General also proposed new legislation to amend the state's existing data breach notification law.[38] Notably, the proposed legislation would expand the definition of "private information" and apply to any entity that holds the private information of New Yorkers, even if that entity does not conduct regular business in the state.[39]

The shifting legal landscape governing cybersecurity may itself be considered a cyber "vulnerability" for a company. Boards need to be cognizant of their companies' compliance obligations, but that is easier said than done. Companies today operate in a fragmented system of cybersecurity regulation.

State, federal, and foreign regulators all come with their own rules and guidance. Certain states, such as California and New York, have taken a particularly aggressive tack in recent years to regulate and enforce cybersecurity standards within their jurisdictional limits. On the federal level, agencies such as the FTC and SEC are on the vanguard of cybersecurity enforcement within their own designated areas of focus and guidance, as well.

The European Union, for its part, recently implemented its General Data Protection Regulation, which imposes reporting and other requirements on companies that collect credit card data or other personal information from EU citizens.[40]

Boards should ensure their companies continue to comply with the latest array of state and federal laws and regulations concerning cybersecurity. This is especially true for companies in certain industries that are frequently targeted by cyber criminals (*e.g.*, financial institutions), and those that handle sensitive personal information, such as personally identifiable information, financial information, or protected health information, as these companies are often subject to scrutiny by regulators and legislators. One obvious first step for the board may be to ask the company's general counsel and CISO to brief the board regularly on legislative developments and provide their recommendations. With many law firms growing their data privacy and cybersecurity practices, companies can also draw on the expertise of outside counsel to develop individualized programs to manage cybersecurity risk, in view of the company's needs.

Boards can also be valuable weapons in combating "compliance fatigue," in which personnel performing the day-to-day compliance functions lose sight of the broader picture as they navigate disparate, daily demands and multiple moving targets. It is important to "check the boxes," but that is not enough. With their high-level perspective and status, boards can play a major role in encouraging management to think critically and innovatively when it comes to improving existing processes and cybersecurity measures. In the end, boards should try to ensure that the lion's share of the company's effort is spent on actual cybersecurity, and not on merely demonstrating compliance.

Conclusion

To implement an effective cybersecurity program, a director should understand the full range of cyber risks facing his or her company and encourage management to develop appropriate strategies tailored to the company's specific needs and goals. Any effective cyber program includes careful planning, smart delegation, and a system for monitoring compliance—all of which directors should own. It's no longer a question of whether a company will be attacked but more a question of when—and what the company is going to do about it. Smart network surveillance, early warning indicators, multiple layers of defense, and learning from past events are all critical components of true cyber resilience. When things go wrong, whether in a major or minor way, the ability to quickly identify and respond to a problem will determine the company's ultimate recovery. Cybersecurity cannot be guaranteed, but a timely and appropriate reaction can.

Directors' Cyber Checklist

Risk Assessment - Evaluate the Existing Cybersecurity Risks, and Prioritize

- ☐ Determine most valuable assets
- ☐ Seek effective strategies to protect them
- ☐ Review cybersecurity budget for appropriateness

Assess Corporate Culture and Set the Right Example

- ☐ C-suite and board must be more than involved, they should set the tone

- ☐ Training should be engaging
- ☐ Culture should be based on teamwork not surveillance

Develop Strategies and Internal Systems to Manage Cyber Risk

- ☐ Evaluate effectiveness of internal systems and controls
- ☐ Participate in selecting key cybersecurity personnel
- ☐ Make sure cybersecurity personnel have board access
- ☐ Understand and develop metrics for evaluating cybersecurity effectiveness
- ☐ Take a hard look at escalation protocols
- ☐ Request a security scorecard
- ☐ Develop an incident response plan
- ☐ Test the plan. Consider simulated cyberattacks

Understand Disclosure Requirements and Third-Party Considerations

- ☐ Review disclosures with an eye toward cybersecurity
- ☐ Put mitigating controls in place for third-party contracts
- ☐ Review cyber insurance coverage

Stay on Top of Developments

- ☐ Regularly reassess your cyber plan in light of the shifting legal landscape
- ☐ Initiate standing review of cyber program on at least a quarterly basis
- ☐ Task general counsel and/or CISO with briefing board on regulatory developments
- ☐ Leverage preexisting relationships with outside counsel

Notes

1 *Roel Campos is a former SEC Commissioner who practices SEC securities enforcement defense and regulation law as a partner at Hughes Hubbard & Reed LLP, and regularly advises boards of directors on securities issues. David X Martin is a well-known risk and business cybersecurity expert. Roel and David serve as co-chairs of the Directors and Chief Risk Officers Group (DCRO) Cyber Risk Governance Council. Together, their collaboration in this article has produced a practical common sense approach, with the necessary legal background, to be useful to directors and management professionals to assist in evaluating the cybersecurity program at a company.*

The authors would like to thank Alyssa Johnson and Elizabeth Solander, also of Hughes Hubbard & Reed LLP, for their significant contributions to this article.

The opinions expressed herein are those of the author(s) and do not necessarily reflect the views of Hughes Hubbard & Reed LLP or its clients. This article is for general information purposes. Nothing in this article is intended to be legal advice nor should be relied upon as legal advice.

2 *See* Prepared Testimony of Richard F. Smith before the U.S. House Committee on Energy and Commerce Subcommittee on Digital Commerce and Consumer Protection (Oct. 3, 2017).

3 *See e.g.,* Bloomberg News, *Equifax Says 2.5 Million More Americans May Be Affected by Hack* (Oct. 2, 2017), https://www.bloomberg.com/news/articles/2017-10-02/urgent-equifax-2-5-million-more-americans-may-be-affected-by-hack.

4 *See* Statement on Cybersecurity by Chairman Jay Clayton (Sept. 20, 2017), https://www.sec.gov/news/public- statement/statement-clayton-2017-09-20.

5 *See e.g.,* Newsweek, *HBO Cyberattack Is "Seven Times Worse" than the Sony Hack* (Aug. 2, 2017), http://www.newsweek.com/hbo-cyberattack-sony-hack-leak-game-thrones-645450.

6 *See* The Guardian, *Deloitte Hit By Cyber-attack Revealing Clients' Secret Emails* (Sept. 25, 2017), https://www.theguardian.com/business/2017/sep/25/deloitte-hit-by-cyber-attack-revealing-clients-secret-emails.

7 *Id.*

8 *See* N.Y. Times, *Uber Hid 2016 Breach, Paying Hackers to Delete Stolen Data* (Nov. 21, 2017),https://www.nytimes.com/2017/11/21/technology/uber-hack.html?mtrref=www.google.com&gwh=34D070015500C54F741A1922ED2C7834&gwt=pay.

9 *See* Press Release, *Equifax Board Releases Findings of Special Committee Regarding Stock Sale by Executives* (Nov. 3, 2017), https://investor.equifax.com/news-and-events/news/2017/11-03-2017-124511096.

10 Time, *Equifax Says You Won't Surrender Your Right to Sue by Asking for Help After Massive Hack* (Sept. 11, 2017), http://time.com/4936081/equifax-data-breach-hack/.

11 *See* Verizon, 2013 Data Breach Investigations Report 13 (2013), http://www.verizonenterprise.com/resources/reports/rp_data-breach-investigations-report-2013_en_xg.pdf.

12 *Id.*

13 Verizon, 2017 Data Breach Investigations Report 3, http://www.verizonenterprise.com/verizon-insights-lab/dbir/2017/ (2017).

14 *Id.*

15 *See* N.Y. Times, *Security Breach and Spilled Secrets Have Shaken the N.S.A. to Its Core* (Nov. 12, 2017), https://www.nytimes.com/2017/11/12/us/nsa-shadow-brokers.html.

16 National Institute of Standards and Technology, Framework for Improving Critical Infrastructure Cybersecurity (Feb. 12, 2014), https://www.nist.gov/sites/default/files/documents/cyberframework/cybersecurity-framework-021214.pdf.

17 *Id.* at 8-9.

18 OCIE Risk Alert, Observations from Cybersecurity Examinations (Aug. 7, 2017), https://www.sec.gov/files/observations-from-cybersecurity-examinations.pdf.

19 *Id.* at 1.

20 *Id.* at 3-4.

21 *Id.* at 3.

22 *See* Bloomberg BNA, *Corporate Cyber Risk Disclosures Jump Dramatically in 2017* (July 26, 2017), https://www.bna.com/corporate-cyber-risk-n73014462313/.

23 *Compare* Testimony on "Oversight of the U.S. Securities and Exchange Commission" by Jay Clayton before the Committee on Banking, Housing and Urban Development of the United States Senate (Sept. 26, 2017), https://www.banking.senate.gov/public/_cache/files/929816e6-9372-404f-ba97- c9d9ed453501/ADC20EE6B81BD706BEE66812F71FADDB.clayton-testimony-9-26-17.pdf, at 3 (testifying the SEC "believe[s] the intrusion did not result in unauthorized access to personally identifiable information"), *with* Press Release, Chairman Clayton Provides Update on Review of 2016 Cyber Intrusion Involving EDGAR System (Oct. 2, 2017),

https://www.sec.gov/news/press-release/2017-186 (observing the breach resulted in the unauthorized disclosure of names, dates of birth, and social security numbers of two individuals).

24 *See* SEC Division of Corporation Finance, CF Disclosure Guidance: Topic No. 2, Cybersecurity (Oct. 13, 2011), https://www.sec.gov/divisions/corpfin/guidance/cfguidance-topic2.htm

25 Reuters, *FTC says it is evaluating 'serious issues' raised in Uber's handling of a data breach* (Nov. 22, 2017), https://www.reuters.com/article/us-uber-cyberattack-ftc/ftc-says-it-is-evaluating-serious-issues-raised-in-ubers-handling-of-a-data-breach-idUSKBN1D-M2EC.

26 *See e.g.*, National Conference of State Legislatures, *Security Breach Notification Laws* (Apr. 21, 2017), http://www.ncsl.org/research/telecommunications-and-information-technology/security-breach-notification-laws.aspx.

27 *See e.g.*, Wall Street Journal, *Home Depot's 56 Million Card Breach Bigger than Target's* (Sept. 18, 2014), https://www.wsj.com/articles/home-depot-breach-bigger-than-targets-1411073571.

28 N.Y. Times, *Panama Papers Show How Rich United States Client Hid Millions Abroad* (June 5, 2016), https://www.nytimes.com/2016/06/06/us/panama-papers.html?mtrref=www.google.com.

29 N.Y. Times, *Paradise Papers Shine Light on Where the Elite Keep Their Money* (Nov. 5, 2017), https://www.nytimes.com/2017/11/05/world/paradise-papers.html.

30 Wall Street Journal, *Regulators Fret About Cyber Risk After SEC Hack* (Oct. 3, 2017), https://www.wsj.com/articles/regulators-fret-about-cyber-risk-after-sec-hack-1507049048.

31 Wall Street Journal, *Insurance Grows for Cyberattacks* (Sept. 17, 2017), https://www.wsj.com/articles/insurance- grows-for-cyberattacks-1505700360.

32 *See* IBM Release, 2017 Ponemon Cost of Data Breach Study, https://www.ibm.com/security/data-breach.

33 Target Corp., 2016 Annual Report 44 (2017), https://corporate.target.com/_media/TargetCorp/annualreports/2016/pdfs/Target-2016-Annual-Report.pdf?ext=.pdf.

34 Bloomberg Technology, *FedEx Cuts Profit Forecast on $300 Million Hit from Cyberattack* (Sept. 19, 2017), https://www.bloomberg.com/news/articles/2017-09-19/fedex-cuts-profit-outlook-on-300-million-blow-from-cyberattack.

35 *Id.*

36 N.Y. COMP. CODES R. & REGS. tit. 23, § 500 (2017).

37 N.Y. COMP. CODES R. & REGS. tit. 23, § 201 (proposed Sept. 18, 2017).

38 Stop Hacks and Improve Electronic Data Security Act (SHIELD Act), Senate Bill S6933, 2017-2018 Reg. Sessions (N.Y. Nov. 1, 2017).

39 *Id.* § 3.

40 Regulation (EU) 2016/679 of the European Parliament and of the Council of 27 April 2016.

INDEX

application programming interfaces (APIs), 7
applying CyRM^{SM}, 83
assessment of current position, 77
Atlanta, (city of) attack, 71

building a more effective cybersecurity defense, 21
    consider methods to transfer cyber risks, 24
    recover and remember, 23
    solve the problem, 23
    sound the alarm, 22

Capital One breach, 6
CISO role, 34–35, 55–56
cloud exposure, third-party, 6–7, 23, 41
COVID-19 pandemic, 8, 72, 79
cultivate a strong culture to enhance cyber security, 59
    data-centric security, 60
    engage employees in training applications, 61
    get the users involved, 60
    make diversity part of the security culture, 61
The Current Landscape, 5
cybersecurity and remote workers, 6, 8
cybersecurity and trust, 66
cybersecurity audits, 22
Cybersecurity Disclosure Act, 72–73

cybersecurity for senior executives and board members, 29
CyberWellness^{SM}
    a companywide approach, 3, 49, 51, 72
    establish effective governance, 54
    implement management processes for all third-party vendors and suppliers, 55
    Incident Response Plans, 51
    ongoing workforce training and development, 54
    penetration testing, 52
    public relations and legal counsel, 54
    tabletop exercises, 53
    take a step back, 56
CyRM^{SM}
    action points, 45
    and disaster scenarios, 71–72
    three prongs, 3
    as a vital business strategy, 69

data-centric security, 60
data loss prevention (DLP), 60
data masking, 60
data processing, 82
decisions and risk, 77
Deloitte data breach, 47
disasters and CyRM^{SM}, 71–72

emerging threats, 81–83
employees and tracking, 75

encryption, 60
Equifax breach, 5, 29
evaluating risk, 79

Facebook breach, 6
Federal Trade Commission (FTC), 40
First American breach, 6

gather intelligence, anticipate risk, 15
governance, 54, 70

Home Depot breach, 47
Homeland Security's United States
    Computer Emergency
    Readiness Team
    ("US-CERT"), 29
how to think about the future, 75
    applying CyRMSM, 83
    assessment, 77
    emerging threats, 81

incident response plans, 51–52
Interconnectedness of CyRM^{SM} and
    business strategy, 71
IT risks, 27–28
IT strategy, 25–26

Java software, 40

Kaizen (Japanese philosophy of), 80

legal considerations, 24
legal counsel, 54

Meltdown, 7

National Security Agency (NSA), 33

Oracle, 44

Panama Papers scandal, 41
phishing, 61
public relations, 54

Quest Diagnostics breach, 6

risk management, 3, 15–16, 19, 21
rules of the game, 78

SEC's EDGAR Database, 31, 39, 42
Securities and Exchange Commission
    (SEC), 5, 31, 37, 39, 72–73
security and governance, 70
skimming and POS attacks, 33
Sony cyberattack, 9
Spectre, 7

tabletop exercises, 53–54
third party vendors and suppliers, 55–56
trust in cybersecurity, 66
trust will become a competitive
    advantage, 65

unknown risks, 17, 19
US-CERT, 29
US government regulation, 9–10

workforce training, 54–55

Printed in the United States
By Bookmasters